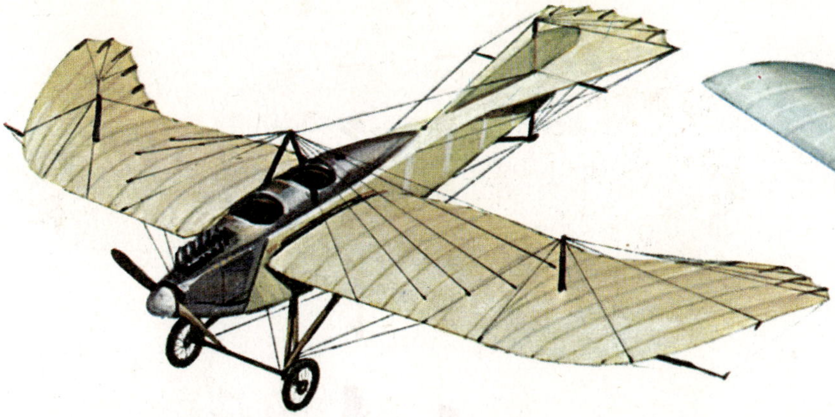

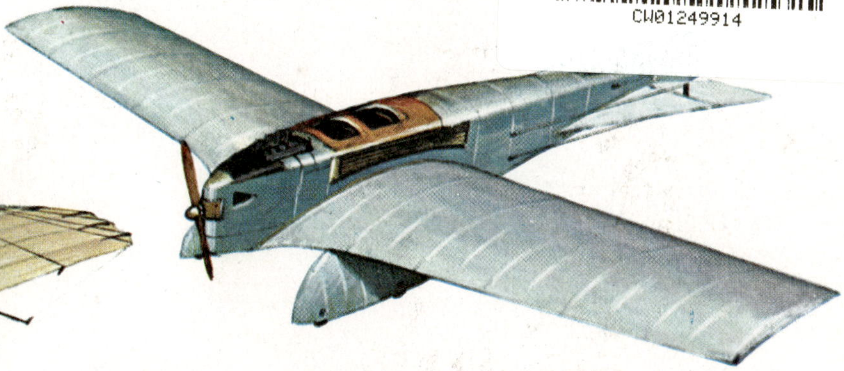

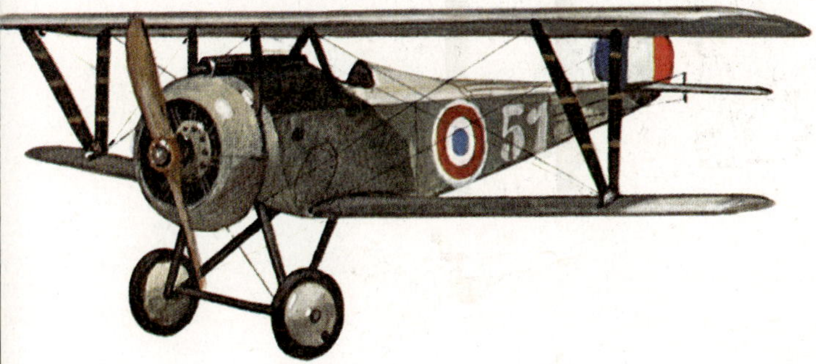
51

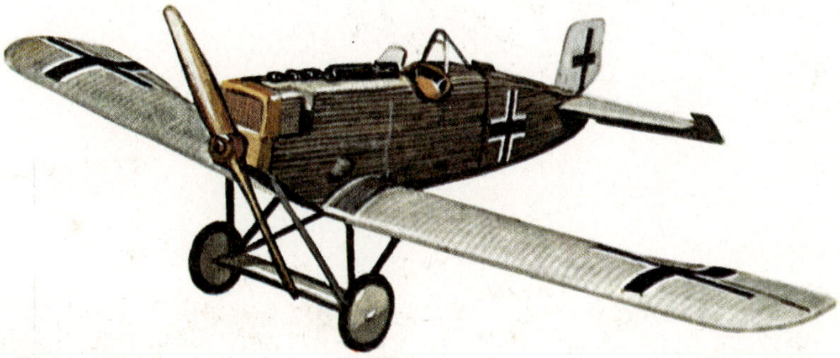

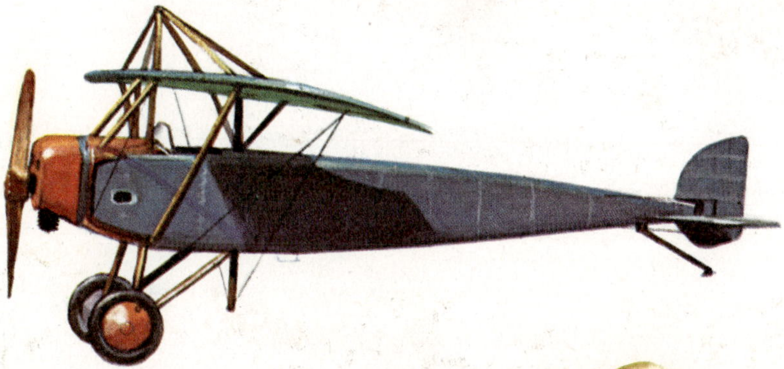

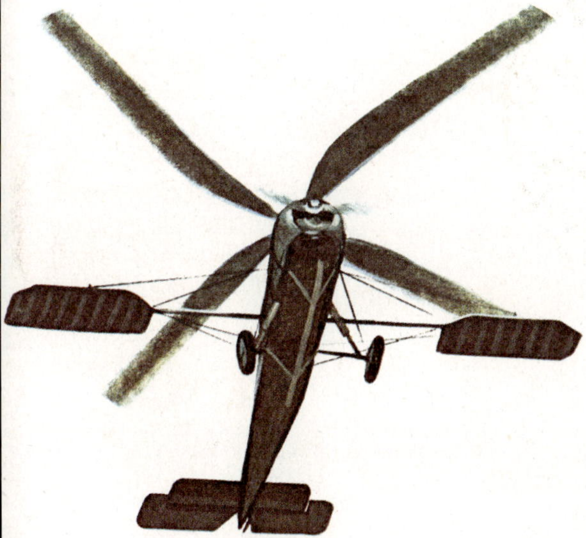

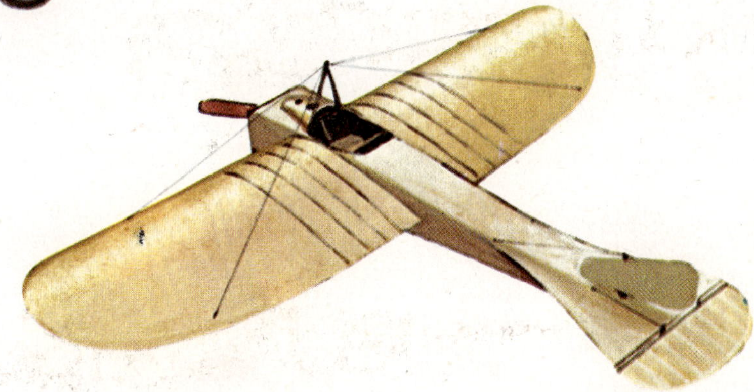

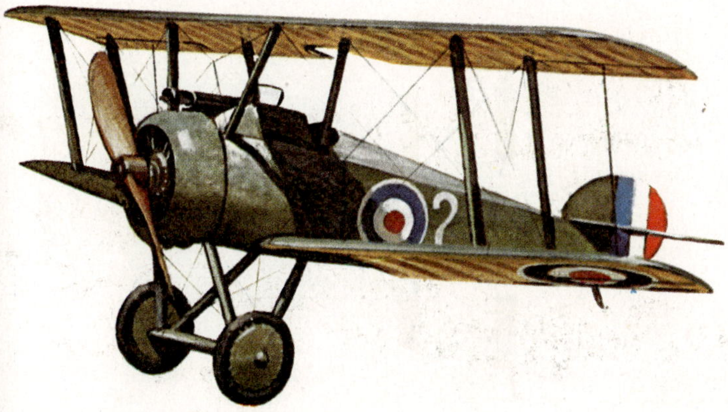

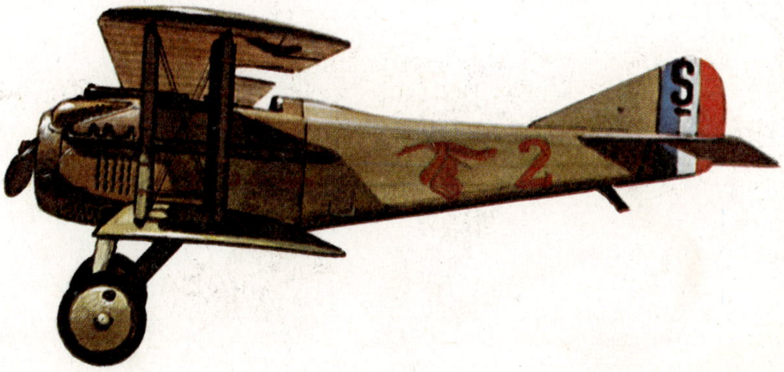
2

library 2000

GREAT INVENTIONS
DISCOVERIES AND INVENTIONS
FAMOUS ARTISTS AND COMPOSERS
SHIPS
WEAPONS OF THE PAST
MODERN WEAPONS
EARLY AIRCRAFT
MODERN AIRCRAFT

Published in Great Britain by Frederick Warne (Publishers) Ltd, London, 1984
Copyright © Ediciones AURIGA, S.A., Madrid, Spain
English translation copyright © Frederick Warne (Publishers) Ltd, 1981

ISBN 0 7232 2771 3

Phototypeset by Tradespools Ltd., Frome, Somerset

Printed in Spain by Sirven S.A.E., Barcelona
Depósito Legal B. 13.051-84

library 2000

Written and illustrated by Vicente Segrelles

Translated by Arthur Butterfield

Early Aircraft

FREDERICK WARNE

CONTENTS

Introduction	7
The age-long yearning to fly	8
Leonardo: light in the darkness	10
Lighter than air: the balloon	12
The coming of the airship	14
Almost an aeroplane	16
The first powered flights	18
The glider	20
Man masters the air	22
Those magnificent men	24
The Zeppelin	26
A soaring of seaplanes	28
Higher and faster	30
Refinements before World War I	32
The first aircraft of World War I	34
The bombers	36
A new breed of fighters	38
The immediate post-war years	40
Civil aviation in the 1920s	42
Warplanes to 1930	44
Warplanes: 1930–35	46
Civil aviation to 1935	48
Giants of the airways	50
Flying fuel tanks	52
Faster still: the flying engine	54
The Schneider Trophy	56
Getting up-to-date	58
Conclusion	60
Important dates	61

INTRODUCTION

The eagle could clearly be seen against the blue of the sky. It flew in wide circles and seemed to be floating on air. Then it suddenly folded its wings and hurtled earthwards in a terrifying dive. Almost scraping the earth, it swooped upwards again in a graceful curve. Now in level flight once more, the eagle could be seen gripping its fresh prey—prey which it would drop in a nest far away and high up in the mountains.

Primitive man was to witness this scene many times, but could never work out how birds, bats, and other winged creatures managed to fly. The secret seemed to lie in the wings. Nevertheless, man—the most intelligent of all God's creatures, the hunter, possessor of weapons, lord of fire, inventor of the wheel—failed miserably in his attempts to imitate the birds of the air. Thus frustrated, man turned to dreaming about flight. His fantasies filled the world with magic winged creatures—one way of satisfying his craving for aerial navigation.

Centuries passed and eventually man did succeed in mastering the air, but it was not done by a birdlike adaptation of his physique and anatomy. He had long ago realized that this was impossible. Instead, he learnt to fly by building an artificial bird and piloting it himself. This book tells the story of the development and evolution of these man-made birds by means of which man gained mastery of the air. It aims to provide the fullest possible picture of the subject without claiming to include every single aircraft ever built. But it does cover all the models that broadly typify the evolution of the aeroplane over the years. This book tells the story of flight from its very beginnings up to the middle of the 1930s, a date that marks the beginning of the modern aircraft industry.

THE AGE-LONG YEARNING TO FLY

True flight was quite beyond primitive man's capabilities. He therefore concluded that it was solely a privilege of the gods who, of course, could always manage the impossible. Not unnaturally then, man came to believe that if a human being did succeed in lifting off, he would be that much nearer to immortality. As a result, the yearning to soar way above the earth became so intense that more than one misguided enthusiast would have sacrificed health and life in the attempt. The stories of these misfortunes may have remained forever engraved in fable, myth, and legend.

The best known of these legends concerns Icarus, son of Daedalus, who escaped from the Cretan labyrinth with feathered wings stuck to his body with wax. Disobeying his father, he flew too near the sun. The wax melted and Icarus plunged to a watery grave.

Did you know...

... that in the tenth century AD the Chinese were already familiar with the comets and quite possibly carried out limited forms of manned flight using gliders made of silk or bamboo, and that they may also have practised a primitive kind of parachute jumping?

This story or legend does not even stand up to the most superficial examination. If there had been a trace of fact in the original it has long since been so transformed as to make it quite unbelievable. Nevertheless, there are more authentic ancient records of flights that may have occurred in China. Though garbled, these indicate the distinct possibility that some kind of flight may indeed have taken place centuries ago.

Among the many existing man-made images of winged deities, here are some that represent various epochs and civilizations. On the right is the Egyptian goddess Isis, copied from the sarcophagus of Rameses III. Below left is a clay impression of an ancient Assyrian seal; and on the right is a detail from a Greek vase in which Sleep and Death are both winged.

On the left is the Winged Victory of Samothrace, a famous Greek sculpture commemorating a naval victory that took place in 200 BC.

On the right is a picture of a Western winged divinity: a traditional angel, so often shown with wings. It seems only natural to us to give wings to supernatural figures. It is therefore strange to find that a few Oriental religions discard wings in favour of anti-gravity in order to ascend.

LEONARDO: LIGHT IN THE DARKNESS

It is quite probable that the great Leonardo da Vinci (1452–1519) was the first man to study the mysteries of bird flight and to investigate the possibilities of flying machines.

Leonardo paid special attention to the problem of mechanically flapping wings. These had never been able to sustain flight because of two fundamental fallacies. The first lay in the belief that birds flap their wings from front to back. The second was a failure to realize that the human body and heart do not possess the strength and rhythmic activity necessary to allow man to hoist himself into the air by his own efforts. If only Leonardo had devoted more time to designing gliders, as he was to do rather too late in his life, the history of aviation might have been different.

In spite of all this, Leonardo's genius stands in stark contrast to the crazy ideas of his contemporaries and even to the beliefs of many of those who came after him. For this reason it can be justifiably stated that Leonardo's achievements shine like a dazzling light through a background of total darkness.

Leonardo's first sketches of flying machines date from 1496. His fertile imagination dreamed up movable wings, the parachute, the helicopter and, finally, the glider. He also calculated important technical data such as the surface area of a plane required for lift, as well as designing a monoplane, a biplane and shock absorbers.

In 1670, Francisco de Lana designed an aerial boat suspended from metal balloons whose interiors were vacuums, but he failed to realize that the weight of any metal strong enough to withstand atmospheric pressure would always be greater than that of the air that had previously been extracted from the balloons.

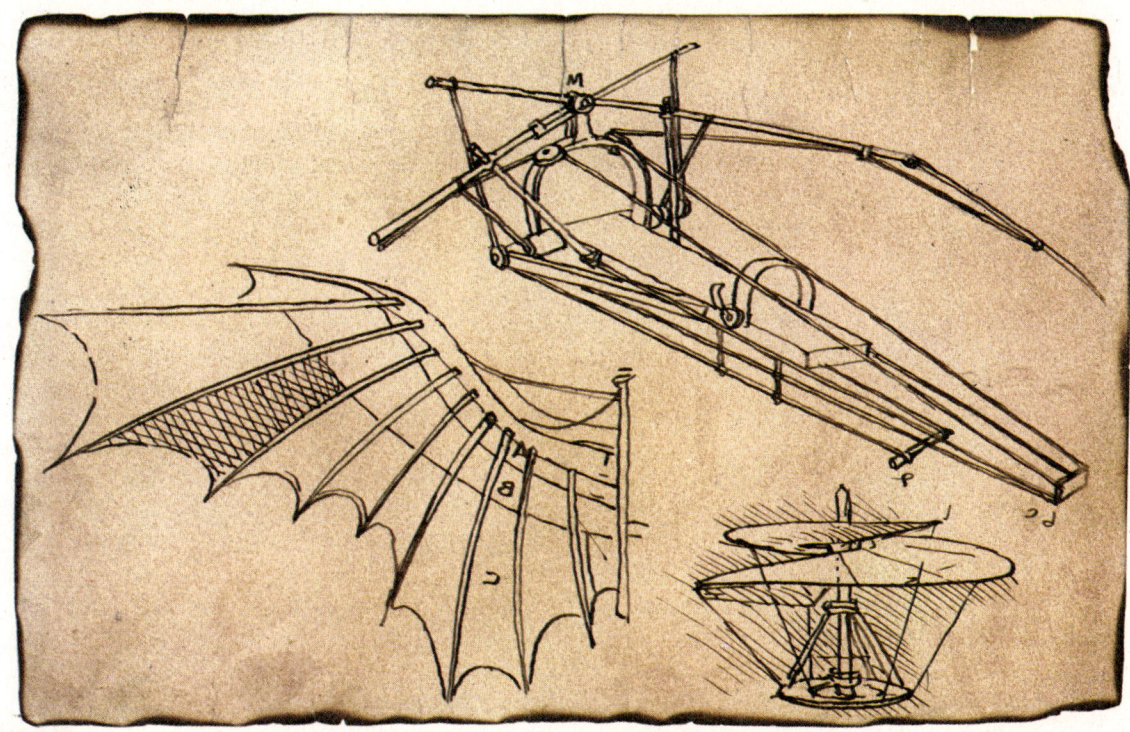

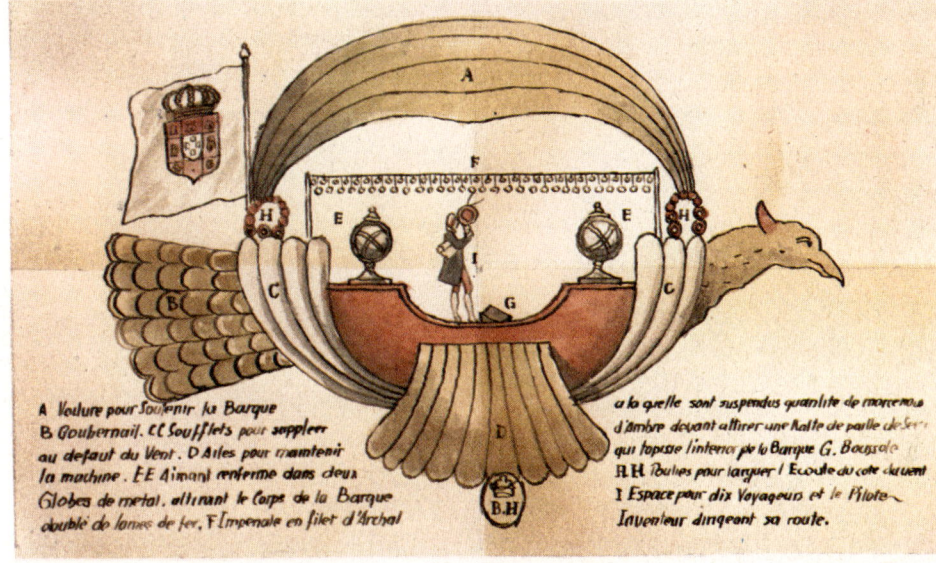

Among the many ingenious ideas for flying vessels was the one above by the Portuguese inventor Bartholomeu de Gusmão (1675–1724) in 1709. It was just as silly as others of that time. We are told that the inventor persuaded the King of Portugal to grant him exclusive rights to its worldwide sale and distribution.

Blanchard's ornithopter—a flying-machine with flapping wings—dates from 1784. Blanchard believed that a man could lift himself into the air by his own unaided physical effort.

At that time many would-be aviators launched themselves into space on home-made wings. They all came to grief in a vertical plunge.

LIGHTER THAN AIR: THE BALLOON

There was no need to find out why smoke always rose into the air. All that was necessary was to imprison the smoke inside a suitable enclosure. But it took thousands of years for this apparently simple idea to register with man. The idea not only had to be thought of but also put into practice. It was in the year 1782 that the idea occurred to one Joseph Montgolfier (1740–1810), a papermaker. This French manufacturer was at home one day idly contemplating the fire blazing in his hearth. Suddenly he began to wonder if the gases which he could see rising up the chimney could not be harnessed to lift an object. As an experiment he made a small silk bag and burnt some paper inside the open neck. The bag promptly inflated and rose to the ceiling.

Joseph told his brother Etienne (1745–99) what had happened and the two of them began to experiment in earnest. A year later, the Montgolfier brothers gave their first public showing. This took place at Annonay with a paper globe 30 m in diameter, lined with linen. The globe swiftly rose to a height of 2,000 m. Some months later they released a second balloon, this one carrying several animals. It came down in perfect condition some two kilometres from the starting point. King Louis XVI of France watched the display, which was an outstanding success. In the meantime, the young French physicist Jacques Charles (1746–1823) had succeeded in launching another kind of balloon which, although it resembled that of the Montgolfiers, was somewhat different. He obtained lift not from hot air but by hermetically sealing a lighter-than-air gas inside the balloon itself. The gas he used was hydrogen. Charles had to overcome many problems, including that of finding a leakproof container and the provision of large amounts of hydrogen. Each type of balloon had its rival supporters. Those who supported Charles's idea were unable to control the ascent and descent of their balloon; the Montgolfiers did this merely by lighting or extinguishing the fire. It was this very characteristic that finished off the Montgolfier balloons, because of the great fire hazard. Ironically, the balloons used by sporting balloonists today are all hot air machines.

The first manned flight in history took place on 21 November 1783. The third gigantic Montgolfier balloon winged its majestic way over the heads of an expectant multitude. It was crewed by Pilâtre de Rozier and the Marquis of Arlandes. The Parisians must have been duly impressed.

On the left is the Montgolfier balloon carrying a sheep, a rooster, and a duck. They were housed in a cage attached to the balloon and were the forerunners of the dogs and chimpanzees launched into space in our own day.

On the right is the first of the manned Charles balloons. It took off ten days after the Montgolfier balloon, with resounding success. It ascended from the Tuileries in Paris and carried its inventor and one of the Robert brothers—the man who eventually overcame the problem of making a leakproof envelope for the balloon.

Jean-Pierre Blanchard (1753–1809) made the first air crossing of the English Channel in this balloon in 1785. The trip was not without its difficulties, caused by a gas leak.

Jean François Pilâtre de Rozier (1756–85) tried to balloon across the English Channel. In order to overcome the problems that had beset Blanchard, he built a hybrid balloon with a container filled with hydrogen above and a cylinder of hot air beneath. In this way he hoped to combine the best features of both systems, but he only succeeded in retaining the worst: the inflammability of one and the quick spread of the other. At a height of 500 m the whole contraption caught fire and Pilâtre and his companion, P. A. Romain, were burnt to death.

The first parachute descent was made in 1797 by André Garnerin (1769–1823). He dropped from a balloon.

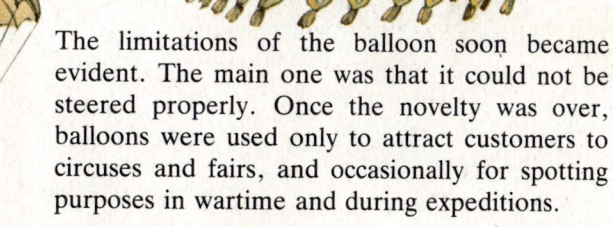

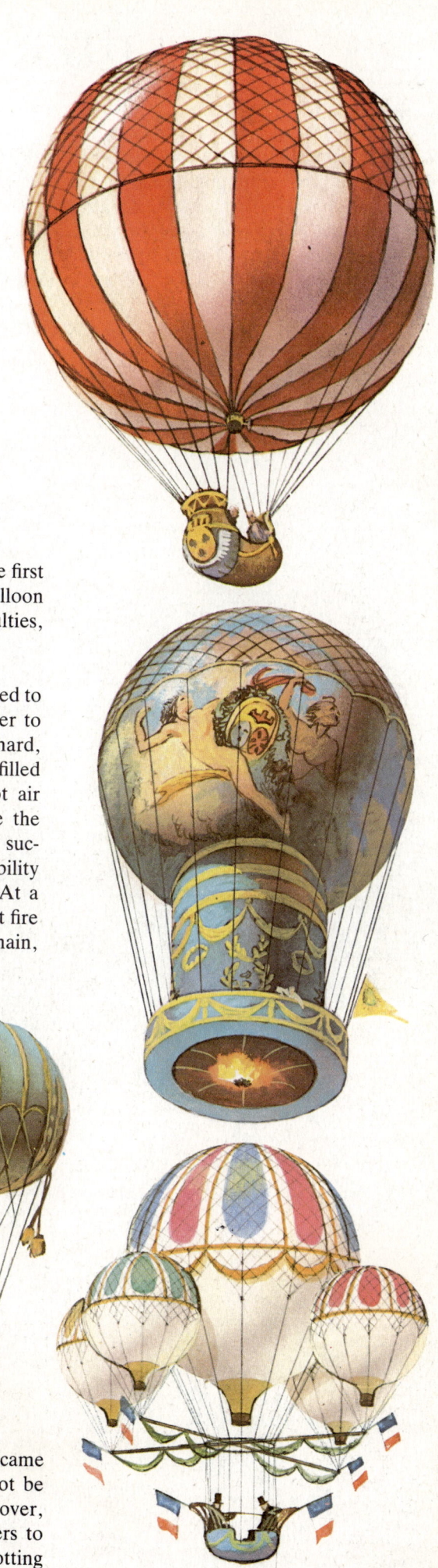

The limitations of the balloon soon became evident. The main one was that it could not be steered properly. Once the novelty was over, balloons were used only to attract customers to circuses and fairs, and occasionally for spotting purposes in wartime and during expeditions.

13

THE COMING OF THE AIRSHIP

After the original enthusiasm had died down, the early aeronauts, faced with the impossibility of being able to steer their craft to a predetermined point, felt cheated. The balloon in reality was a tiny vessel which floated along at the mercy of the winds. As a result, the pioneers of the air endeavoured to steer their craft by means of almost every known kind of propulsion—oars, sails, wheels, and propellers. But it was all in vain. It looked very much as if there was to be no future for the balloon. After much research it was decided that an elongated balloon would be easier to steer, rather like the hull of a ship. Nevertheless, the *dirigible*, or airship, as this new shape was called, did not become efficient until eventually a powerful but very light propulsion agent enabled the vessel to respond to rudders.

The picture shows *La France*, a dirigible built in 1884 by two French army officers, Charles Renard and A. C. Krebs. This was the first airship that could be steered in any direction, regardless of the wind. It was propelled by an electric motor powered by a group of batteries, which gave it a speed of 23 km an hour. This was the best that could be done at the time, but there was no doubt that the batteries, apart from their poor range, also strictly limited the vessel's cargo-carrying capacity.

Did you know...

... that at one time people seriously considered using captive eagles to pull balloons through the air?

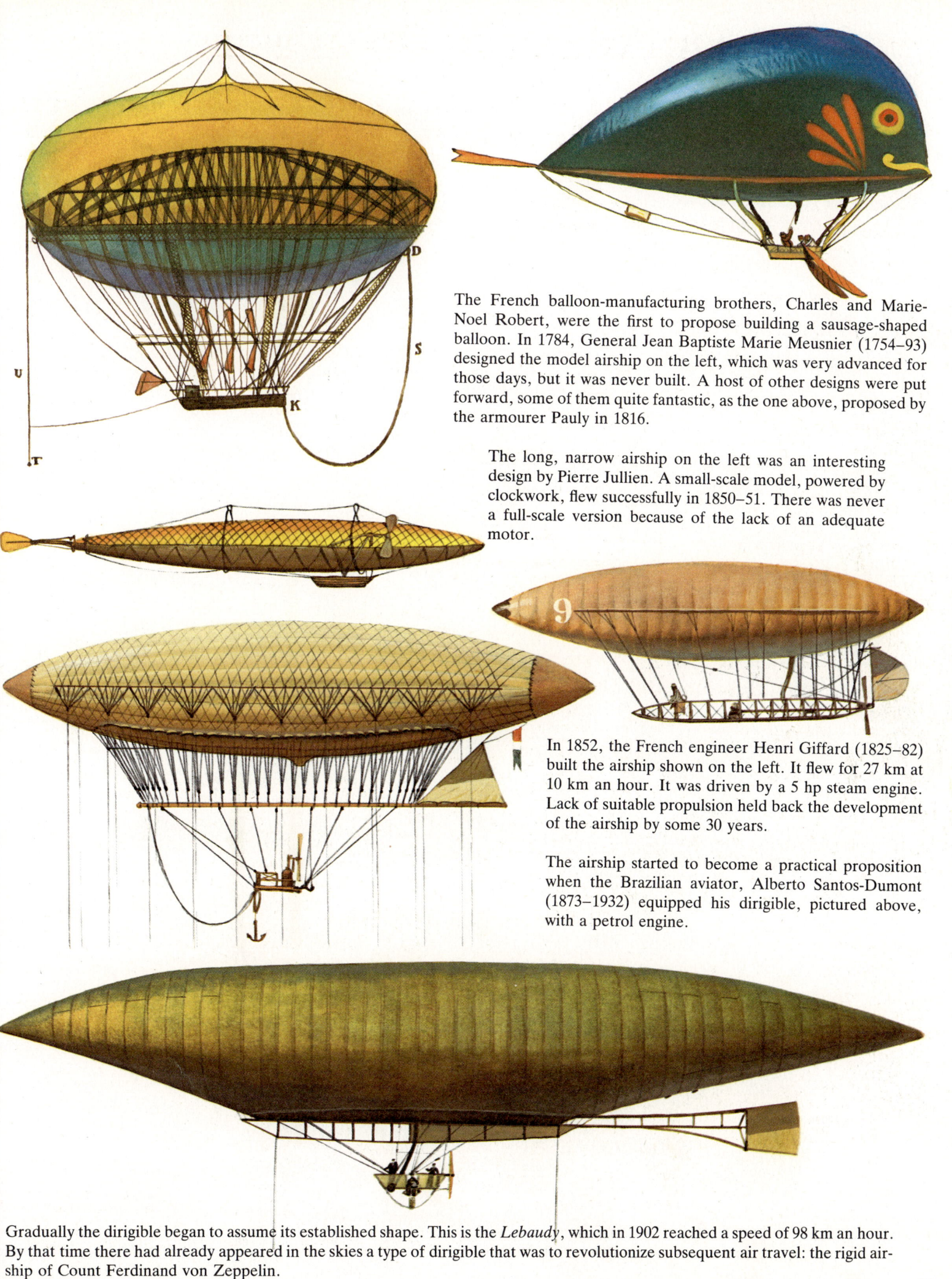

The French balloon-manufacturing brothers, Charles and Marie-Noel Robert, were the first to propose building a sausage-shaped balloon. In 1784, General Jean Baptiste Marie Meusnier (1754–93) designed the model airship on the left, which was very advanced for those days, but it was never built. A host of other designs were put forward, some of them quite fantastic, as the one above, proposed by the armourer Pauly in 1816.

The long, narrow airship on the left was an interesting design by Pierre Jullien. A small-scale model, powered by clockwork, flew successfully in 1850–51. There was never a full-scale version because of the lack of an adequate motor.

In 1852, the French engineer Henri Giffard (1825–82) built the airship shown on the left. It flew for 27 km at 10 km an hour. It was driven by a 5 hp steam engine. Lack of suitable propulsion held back the development of the airship by some 30 years.

The airship started to become a practical proposition when the Brazilian aviator, Alberto Santos-Dumont (1873–1932) equipped his dirigible, pictured above, with a petrol engine.

Gradually the dirigible began to assume its established shape. This is the *Lebaudy*, which in 1902 reached a speed of 98 km an hour. By that time there had already appeared in the skies a type of dirigible that was to revolutionize subsequent air travel: the rigid airship of Count Ferdinand von Zeppelin.

ALMOST AN AEROPLANE

The years passed and the prospect of ever getting a heavier-than-air machine to fly looked depressingly black. However, towards the end of the eighteenth century along came the British inventor Sir George Cayley (1773–1857), regarded by many as the father of modern aviation.

Cayley went back to square one and saw clearly that the future of flight lay not in beating wings nor in other movable parts propelled by human muscle, but in a fixed wing machine controlled by means of rudders placed aft. Here is a highly significant statement of his, which gives the measure of the man. He said, 'This is the problem: to provide a plane surface of a given weight, driven by a force strong enough to overcome wind resistance; with wings set at an angle to ensure lateral stability; a rudder for controlling vertical movement and another for direction, and powered by engines equipped with propellers.'

Basing his design on Cayley's principles, William Samuel Henson produced a very advanced machine with the object of founding the world's first air transport company. His publicity did at least revive public interest in aviation.

This was Henson's flying machine *Ariel*, copied from a contemporary leaflet. It was never built, but there is no doubt that it was a practical proposition. Powered by steam, its proportions and arrangement of components were such that Henson might well figure among the greatest of the pioneers of aviation.

Cayley and some of his drawings. The placing of the control surfaces and the curved aerofoil are particularly interesting. He came up with the idea of a curved surface after a series of experiments involving a machine invented by himself, which measured the wind resistance of the various surfaces. Cayley went on to build full-size gliders which, according to some observers, actually flew.

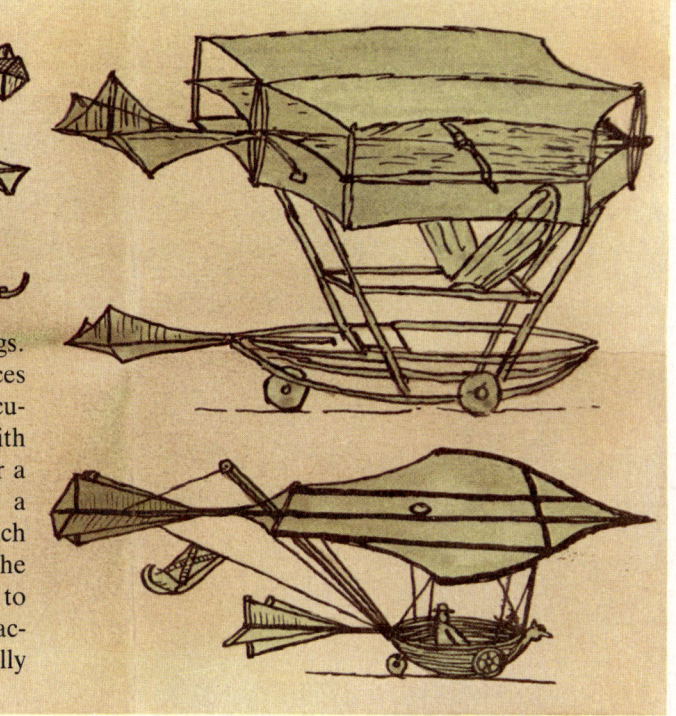

Henson was forced to give up his work because of shortage of cash to build his *Ariel*. His friend and partner, the British engineer John Stringfellow, then went on to experiment with the scale model of *Ariel*, which he had built in collaboration with Henson. He revamped the model and got it to fly, but he too eventually abandoned the project.

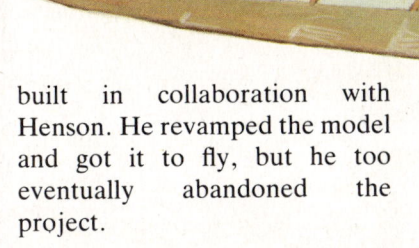

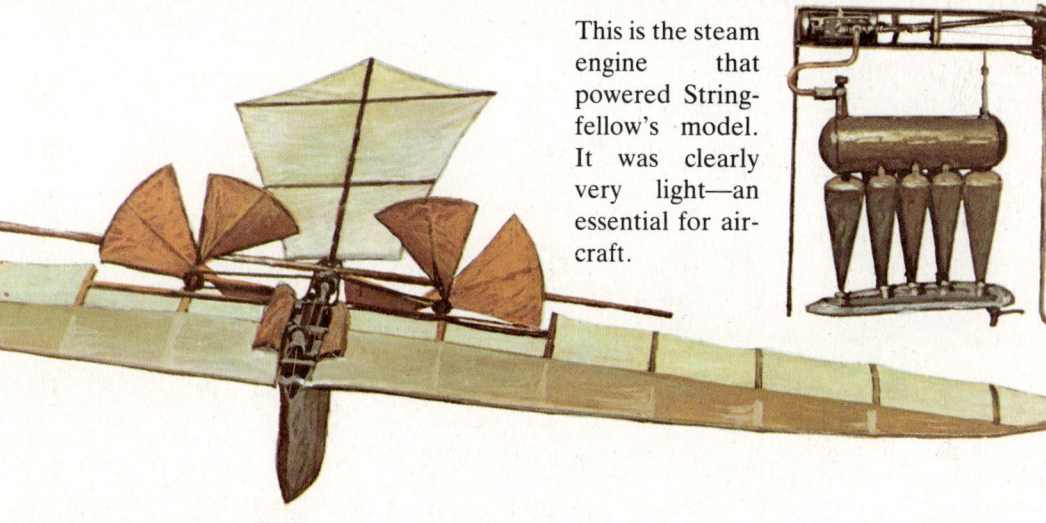

This is the steam engine that powered Stringfellow's model. It was clearly very light—an essential for aircraft.

Another outstanding pioneer was the French inventor Alphonse Pénaud (1850–80). From his early youth he had been interested in aviation. At the age of 20 he began to experiment with models powered by rubber bands. The model shown here flew more than 60 m in 13 seconds, in August 1871. Depressed and disillusioned over lack of funds to build his great flying wing, Pénaud killed himself when he was just 30 years old.

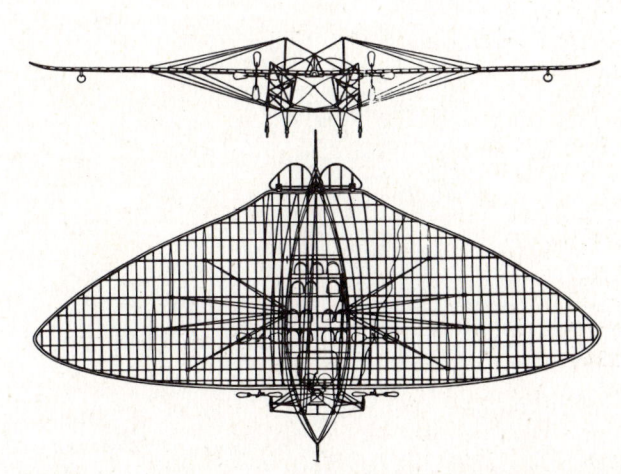

This was Pénaud's flying wing. It incorporated many of the characteristics displayed by today's aircraft. Unfortunately Pénaud was unable to find an engine sufficiently powerful for his machine. This fact must have added to his despair.

THE FIRST POWERED FLIGHTS

Towards the end of the nineteenth century some pioneers had managed a few 'leaps' into the air in their machines. The point was that the weakness of the engines that drove them did not allow the machines to develop sufficient forward thrust to keep them airborne. Perhaps this was just as well, considering the flimsy nature of the craft and the universal ignorance about piloting and aerial manoeuvrability. The Wright brothers were the first to realize that in order to fly properly the first thing one has to do is to learn to fly, regardless. Their experiments with kites and gliders enabled them to learn about the laws of the air and gain experience in manoeuvring.

At that time, the nations that were most advanced in aeronautics each claimed to be the first to establish true flight. But really these were merely prolonged leaps. One of these leaps had dramatic repercussions at the time. It concerned the Frenchman Clément Ader and his *Avion III* pictured here. This machine was built in secret in 1897 and subsidized by the French War Ministry. For purely political reasons, it was claimed that the machine had flown over a certain distance, when actually neither of its wheels had ever left the ground. This was confirmed by an official admission much later.

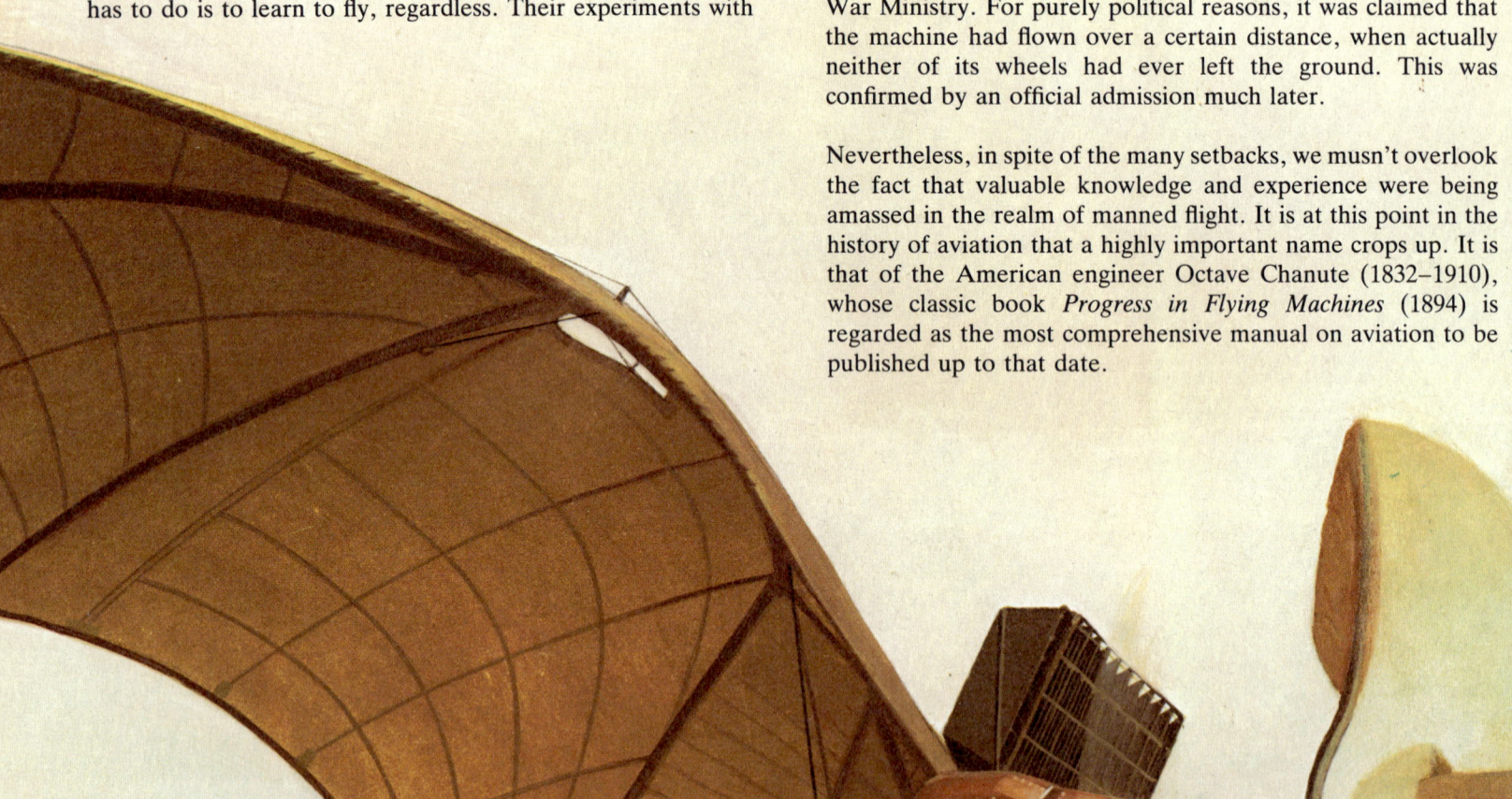

Nevertheless, in spite of the many setbacks, we musn't overlook the fact that valuable knowledge and experience were being amassed in the realm of manned flight. It is at this point in the history of aviation that a highly important name crops up. It is that of the American engineer Octave Chanute (1832–1910), whose classic book *Progress in Flying Machines* (1894) is regarded as the most comprehensive manual on aviation to be published up to that date.

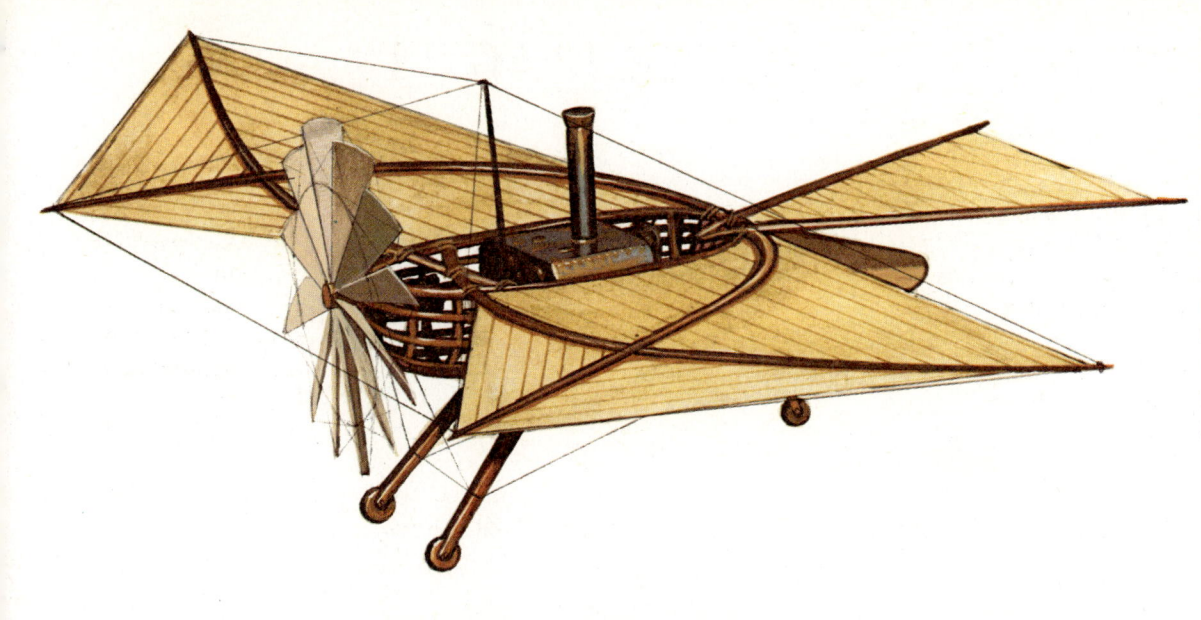

In 1857, Félix Du Temple patented the machine shown on the left. First he built a small-scale model powered by clockwork. Then, in 1874, he developed a steam engine suitable for use with a full-sized version. Under full power, and piloted by a sailor, it rose a little into the air during its brief run. This was the first known flight of a manned aeroplane.

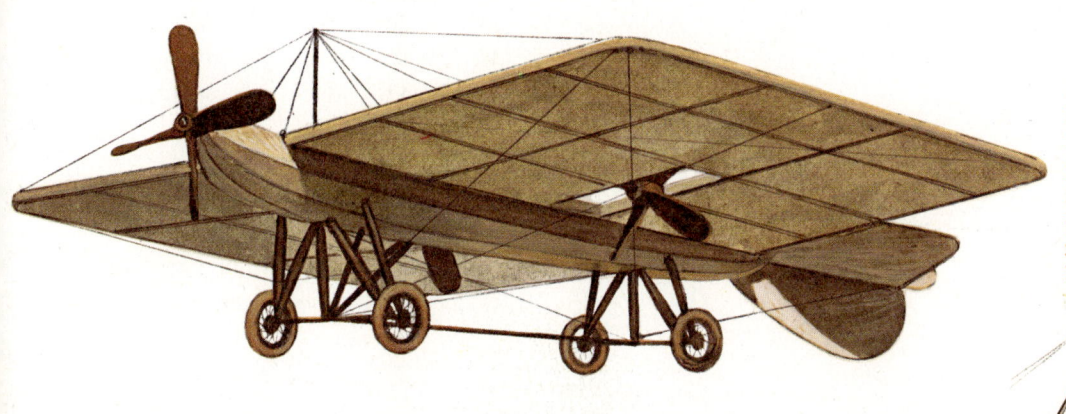

This is the machine built by the Russian inventor Alexander Mozhaiski. In 1884 it was launched from a ramp and managed to stay airborne for some 30 m, although not without a few fits and starts.

Sir Hiram Maxim (1840–1916), the inventor of the machine gun, tried out at his farm in Kent a huge aeroplane, powered by steam. To stop it flying, it was anchored to rails, but it had so much lift that it broke free and flew briefly. It crashed to its destruction in 1894.

In 1893, the Englishman, Horatio Phillips, who had settled for thick aerofoils after experiments in a wind tunnel, managed to lift this extraordinary contraption (with shuttered wings) off a circular track.

The machine above, built by the German inventor Karl Jatho (1873–1933) was perhaps the liveliest before the true flight of the Wright brothers. In November 1903 it made an uncontrolled leap of 60 m.

THE GLIDER

The French sea captain Jean Marie le Bris was very fond of flying. After carefully observing sea birds in flight, he decided to build a fixed-wing glider on the general lines of an albatross. The wings were slightly movable and by this means the inventor hoped to be able to control its flight. He made his first attempt in the autumn of 1856. His method of launching was extremely efficient: he placed the glider on top of a cart pulled by a horse. Standing up in his machine, le Bris gave orders to cast off. As soon as the cart had gathered sufficient speed, he stretched the wings to their maximum width and the machine took off. Unfortunately it was not only the glider that became airborne but also the coachman, who had managed to get a foot caught in the ropes. As soon as he saw what had happened, le Bris folded the wings and dropped back to earth. He continued his experiments for a while but eventually gave up after a long series of failures.

Le Bris's machine is regarded as the first manned glider to fly. But true 'flight' by gliders did not take place until 1891 with the appearance of the German Otto Lilienthal (1849–96). His flights of up to 400 m showed that the conquest of the air was a feasible proposition.

Did you know...

...that in order to build a glider, George Cayley forsook his obsession with kites, and that the extended gliding flights of birds probably suggested exciting possibilities to the inventors of the first heavier-than-air machines?

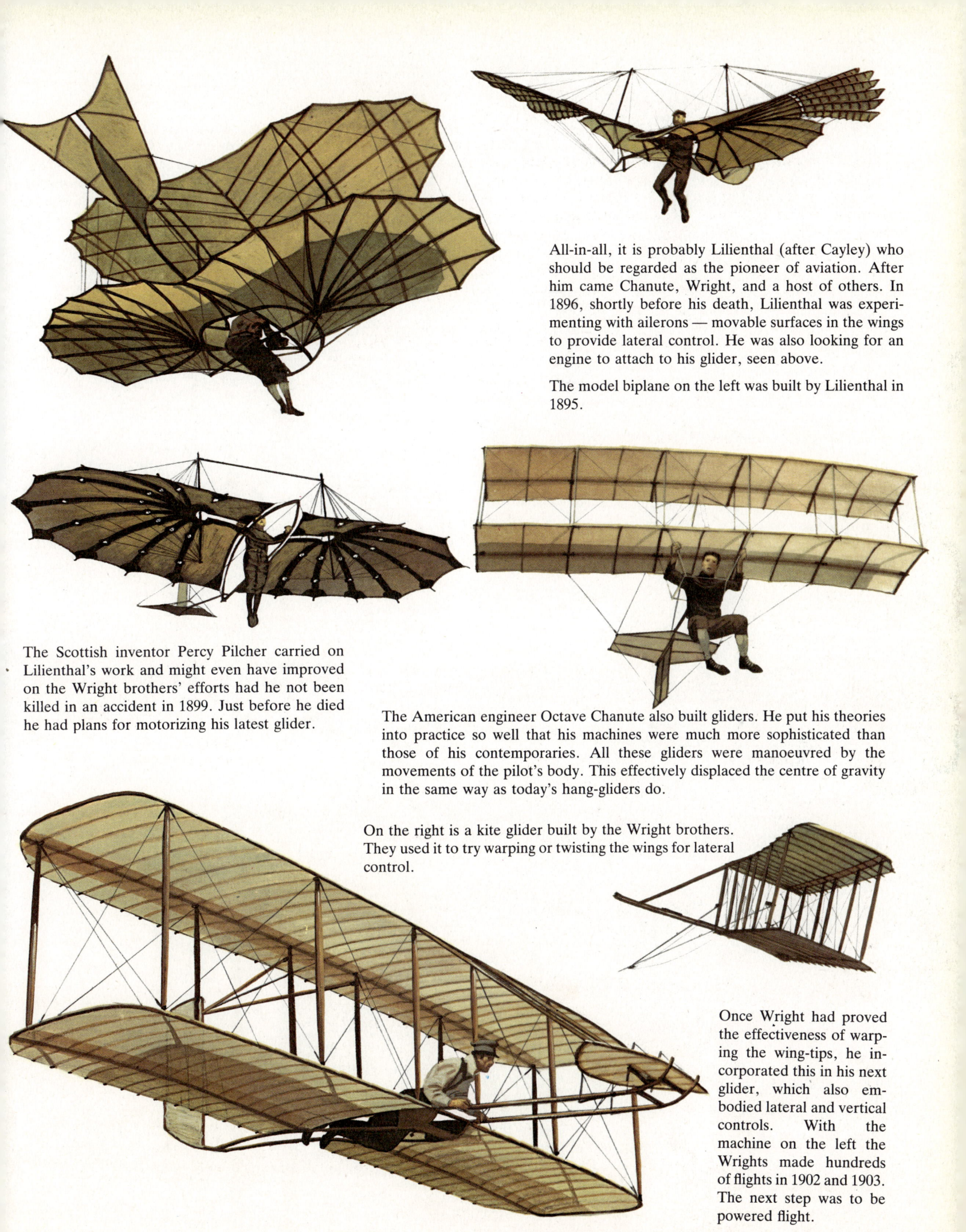

All-in-all, it is probably Lilienthal (after Cayley) who should be regarded as the pioneer of aviation. After him came Chanute, Wright, and a host of others. In 1896, shortly before his death, Lilienthal was experimenting with ailerons — movable surfaces in the wings to provide lateral control. He was also looking for an engine to attach to his glider, seen above.

The model biplane on the left was built by Lilienthal in 1895.

The Scottish inventor Percy Pilcher carried on Lilienthal's work and might even have improved on the Wright brothers' efforts had he not been killed in an accident in 1899. Just before he died he had plans for motorizing his latest glider.

The American engineer Octave Chanute also built gliders. He put his theories into practice so well that his machines were much more sophisticated than those of his contemporaries. All these gliders were manoeuvred by the movements of the pilot's body. This effectively displaced the centre of gravity in the same way as today's hang-gliders do.

On the right is a kite glider built by the Wright brothers. They used it to try warping or twisting the wings for lateral control.

Once Wright had proved the effectiveness of warping the wing-tips, he incorporated this in his next glider, which also embodied lateral and vertical controls. With the machine on the left the Wrights made hundreds of flights in 1902 and 1903. The next step was to be powered flight.

MAN MASTERS THE AIR

In December 1903, the American aviation pioneers, Wilbur (1867–1912) and Orville (1871–1948) Wright managed a flying leap of 260 m in their machine, much greater than anything achieved in Europe. A year later they succeeded in staying airborne for more than half an hour, covering nearly 40 km.

At the beginning of the twentieth century, many thought that all that was needed to fly was a reasonably stable machine with an engine powerful enough to lift it off the ground. But those who already had some gliding experience realized that it was not easy to control a machine in flight. This is where the brothers' know-how came into its own. They realized that with the controls available at that time, flight would be impossible. What was most needed was an effective lateral control because any slight blow could tip the aircraft to one side and send it crashing to the ground. The Wright brothers decided to develop their idea of warping the wing-tips (later superseded by ailerons) and synchronizing rudder and warp. Until that time nobody knew if this would work or not because it had to be proved in flight. As it turned out, systematic research and experiment paid off for the Wrights, and their ideas bore fruit. With this alone, they put America five years ahead of European aviation. But the lure of big business was to lose the brothers their lead. They sold their invention to the big military powers in Europe and, as a result of the necessary secrecy, were virtually unknown to the public. When, in 1908, they came out into the open, they found themselves competing with names such as Voisin, Farman and Antoinette.

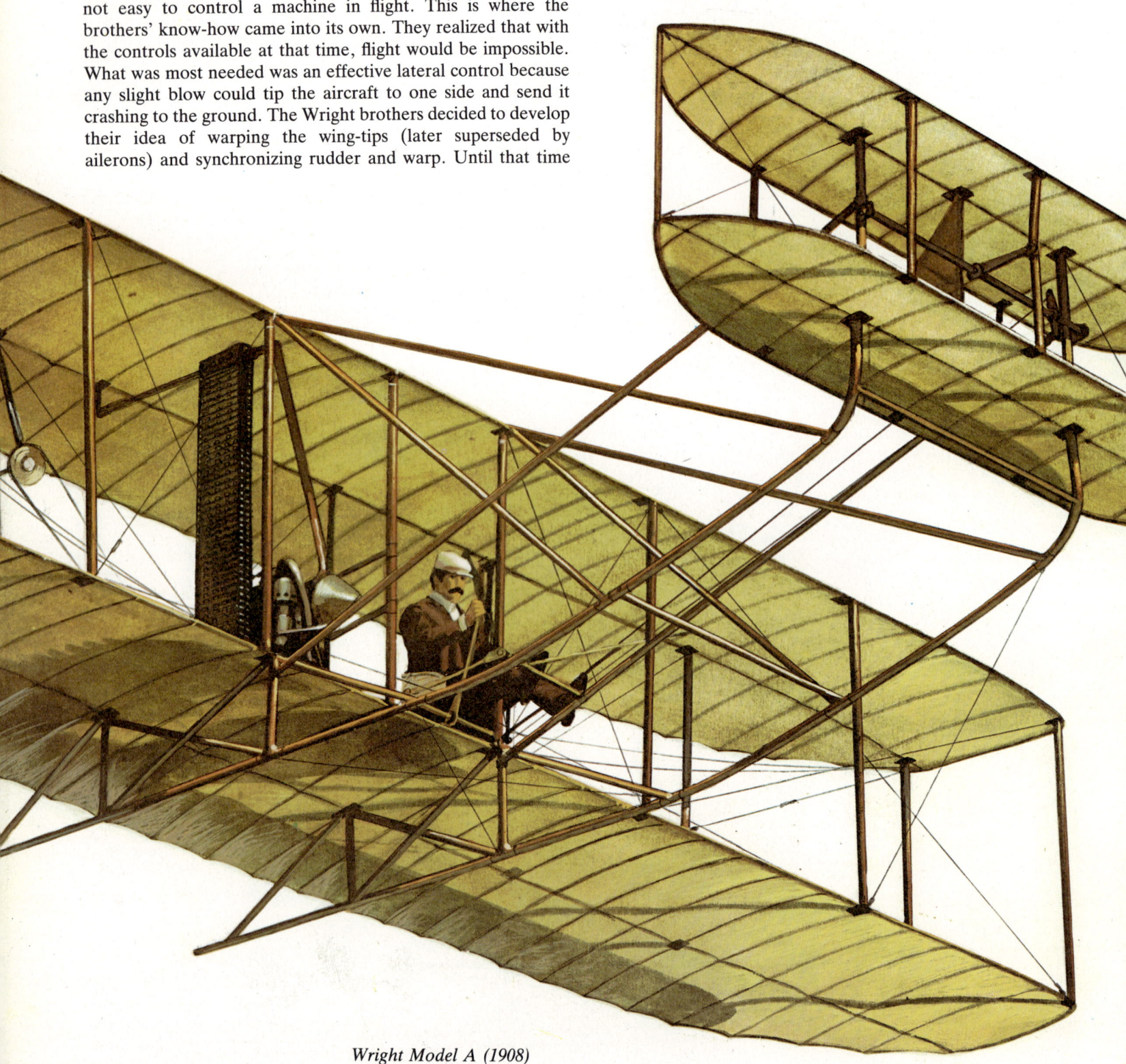

Wright Model A (1908)

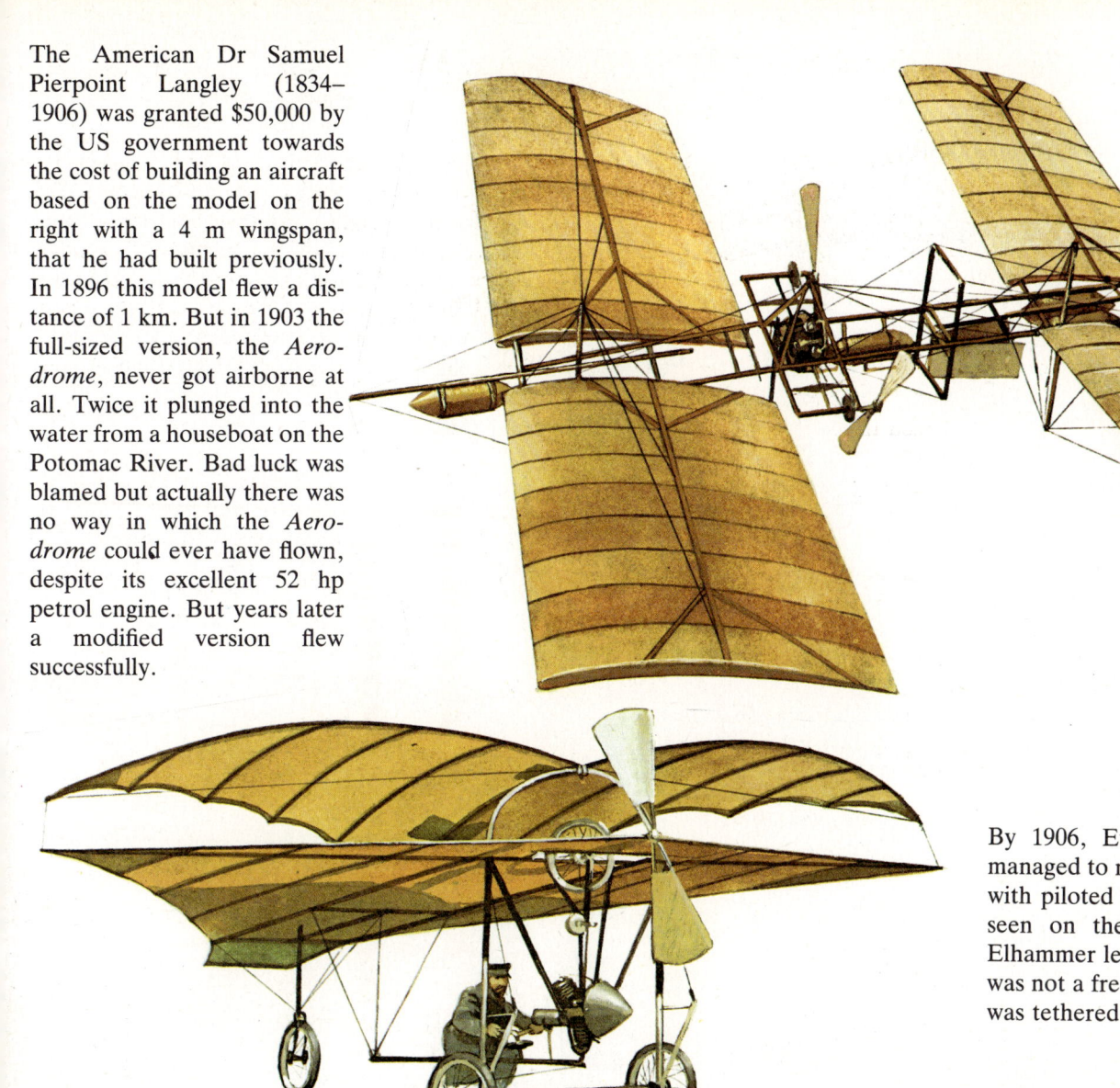

The American Dr Samuel Pierpoint Langley (1834–1906) was granted $50,000 by the US government towards the cost of building an aircraft based on the model on the right with a 4 m wingspan, that he had built previously. In 1896 this model flew a distance of 1 km. But in 1903 the full-sized version, the *Aerodrome*, never got airborne at all. Twice it plunged into the water from a houseboat on the Potomac River. Bad luck was blamed but actually there was no way in which the *Aerodrome* could ever have flown, despite its excellent 52 hp petrol engine. But years later a modified version flew successfully.

By 1906, European aviators had only managed to make more or less long leaps with piloted aircraft. In the kind of kite seen on the left, the Danish airman Elhammer leapt a distance of 45 m. This was not a free flight because the machine was tethered to a post.

In 1906 Santos-Dumont also made an aerial leap in his machine, only this was quite a long leap (220 m at a height of 6 m). This gained him the world's first official airspeed record of more than 40 km an hour. It was a 'canard' type of machine with its tail in front.

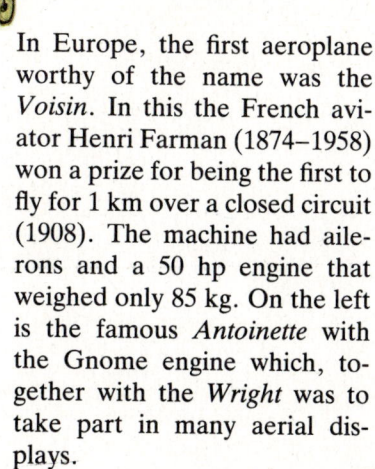

In Europe, the first aeroplane worthy of the name was the *Voisin*. In this the French aviator Henri Farman (1874–1958) won a prize for being the first to fly for 1 km over a closed circuit (1908). The machine had ailerons and a 50 hp engine that weighed only 85 kg. On the left is the famous *Antoinette* with the Gnome engine which, together with the *Wright* was to take part in many aerial displays.

THOSE MAGNIFICENT MEN...

At dawn on 25 July 1909, the French aviator Loius Blériot (1872–1936) managed to fly across the English Channel. This was a feat that nobody thought would come off because Blériot had a poor reputation as a pilot, with a penchant for breaking his aircraft, usually on landing. As a result of his achievement he pocketed £10,000, put up by the *Daily Mail*, plus another 500 francs donated by Ruinart champagne. This money was the prize for being the first airman to fly across the Channel. In addition, his factory received more than a hundred orders for aircraft like his.

Apart from the enormous public popularity that Blériot's feat produced, in competition with Hubert Latham, it also demonstrated that there was a viable future for aviation and that France was one of the outstanding nations connected with it. And to the consternation of a few British admirals and politicians it also showed that would-be invaders could now hop over the ditch that once separated and defended Britain from the rest of Europe.

However, this new science was still in its infancy. Had it not been for a fine drizzle that cooled Blériot's 24 hp Anzani engine, he would never have made it to Dover Castle where, incidentally, his landing could have been improved on.

Did you know...

...that the French engineer Esnault-Pelterie was the only man in the world to have invented and built an aeroplane by himself down to the last nut and bolt and then piloted it himself?

This upsurge of hero-worship of the pioneer airmen by the public resulted in a kind of aviation madness. Many enthusiasts built their own contraptions in search of fame and fortune. Nearly all these wierd machines ended up in spectacular crashes. Two examples, both from 1908, can be seen here, above and to the right.

Robert Esnault-Pelterie, a famous French engineer, fathered a vast number of inventions, among which were the safety belt, the joystick, and tubular steel construction. He built this strange but advanced machine on the left, which flew in 1908.

The first entirely British machine actually to fly was built by a young enthusiast by the name of A. V. Roe, who was later to become the maker of the famous Avro aircraft. His machine, on the left, was a triplane made of wood and brown paper. It boasted a 9 hp JAP engine and flew for 300 m at Wembley in 1909. Roe was threatened with prosecution for this flight, being accused of disturbing the peace—and this was at the time when Blériot was receiving worldwide adulation for his feat. Young Roe deserved praise rather than blame.

On the left is the Levavasseur *Antoinette*, which competed against Blériot's machine over the English Channel. This aircraft was distinguished by its slimness and by its rejection (along with Blériot's) of the Wright's biplane formula.

THE ZEPPELIN

At the beginning of the twentieth century there were three kinds of dirigibles: non-rigid, semi-rigid, and rigid. The non-rigid airship derived its shape from the pressure of gas held within a rubberized outer envelope. The semi-rigid airship was similar to the non-rigid, but it was stiffened with a rigid steel keel. The rigid vessel was essentially a framework of metal girders housed in a rubberized cloth material. This last type had undoubted advantages. It meant that airships of vast size could be built. The interior could be divided up into a number of airtight compartments and, of course, should there be a leak, the great balloon would retain its shape.

The dirigible was invented by Count Ferdinand von Zeppelin (1838–1917) and it immediately displaced all its rivals. Because of its great size, passengers were able to travel in comfort and also had an added feeling of security. This feeling was entirely deceptive, as became obvious in numerous later disasters, for the airship was in reality highly dangerous and vulnerable, especially when filled with hydrogen.

On the left is Zeppelin's first airship, built in 1900. It had an aluminium framework and was 130 m long.

Below is the British airship R34. It was a rigid type, 198 m long. It was the first airship to cross the Atlantic after the *Vimy*'s celebrated crossing in 1919, and it did it in 108 hrs 12 mins, and then made the return crossing in 75 hrs. It showed itself to be a serious rival to the aeroplane.

The *Graf Zeppelin*, the most famous airship of all time, was built in 1928 and was 236 m in length.

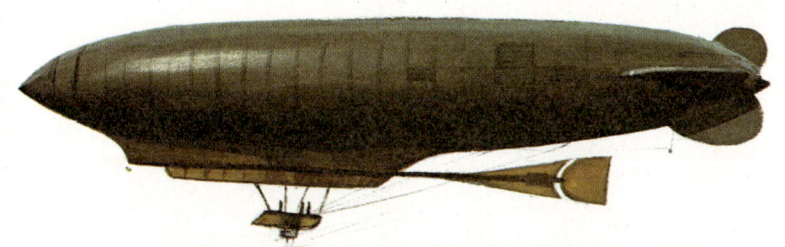

The French, influenced by Santos-Dumont's ideas, decided to build a non-rigid airship, but when this proved incapable of competing with rigid types, it fell into disuse. Above is the *Patrie* of 1906.

The only ones to persist with the non-rigid airship were the Americans, and then only for military purposes. But they also built rigid types and filled these with non-inflammable helium.

The end of the airship era came with the *Hindenburg* disaster. This was an enormous airship, 245 m long, with luxury cabins, dining room, library, its own printing department, and other facilities for its 50 passengers. The catastrophe took place in 1937, just as the great airship was approaching its mooring mast in New Jersey.

A SOARING OF SEAPLANES

We don't know for certain if the pioneer aviators turned to the seaplane because of the reassuring knowledge that they could float on the water in case of a breakdown when flying over the sea, or because they would have a better chance of survival after a bad landing, or because the huge, smooth surfaces of lakes, rivers, and harbours offered ample room for take-off and landing when airfields were virtually non-existent. It is certain, though, that the pilots, just as soon as they could rise from the ground, began to look round for the ideal float for an aeoroplane.

Very soon, the seaplane found an enthusiastic market, both civil and military. Its development paralleled that of the land plane. It reached its peak of importance in the 1930s when ocean travel became commonplace. In 1912 the Schneider Trophy for seaplanes was initiated and became a highly prestigious event.

Although the first take-off from water took place in Europe, it was an American, Glen Hammond Curtiss (1878–1930), the original manufacturer of the flying boat, who in 1911 clearly demonstrated the possibilities of this type of machine.

The Breguet seaplane of 1913 at the moment of take-off

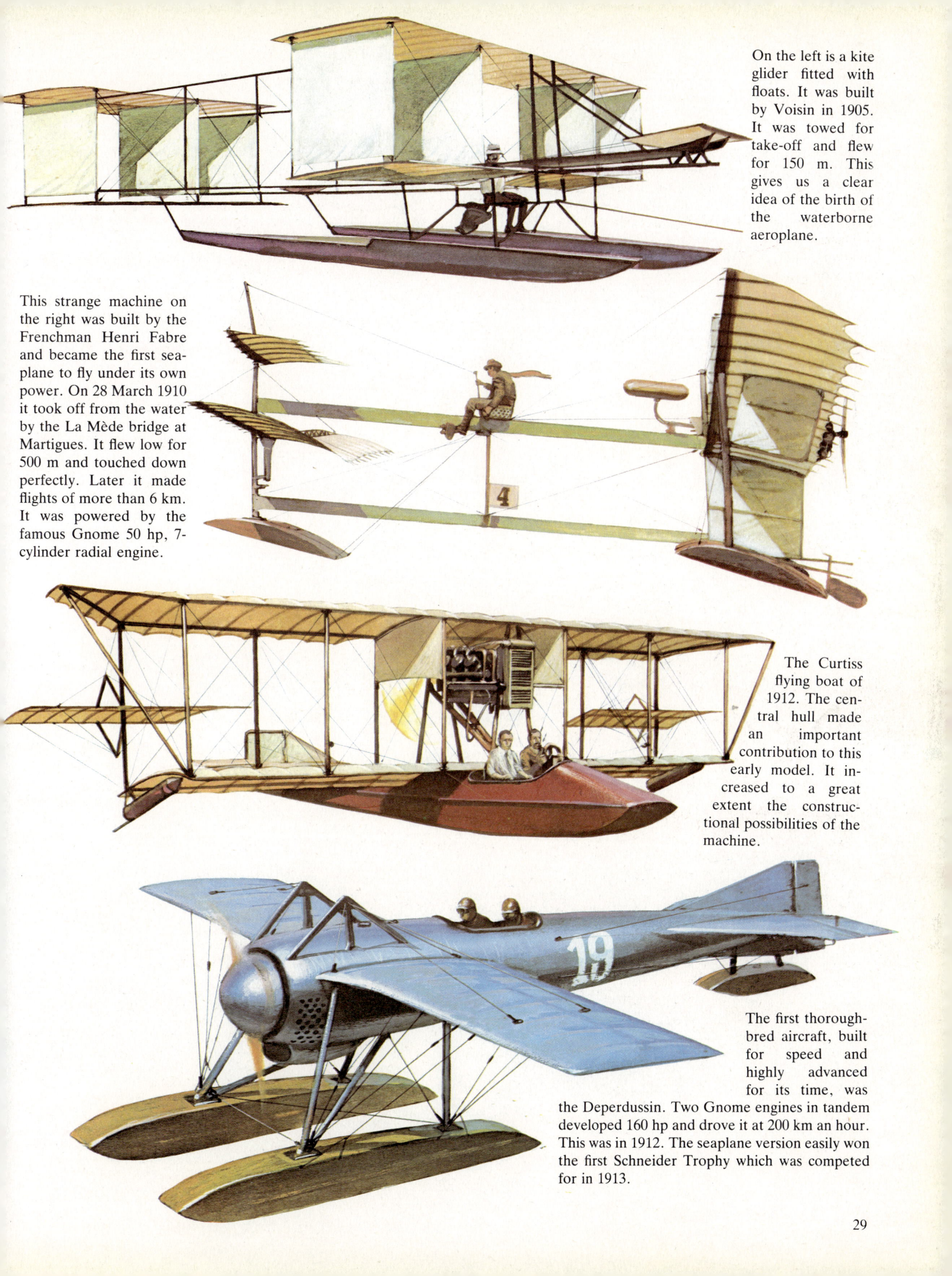

On the left is a kite glider fitted with floats. It was built by Voisin in 1905. It was towed for take-off and flew for 150 m. This gives us a clear idea of the birth of the waterborne aeroplane.

This strange machine on the right was built by the Frenchman Henri Fabre and became the first seaplane to fly under its own power. On 28 March 1910 it took off from the water by the La Mède bridge at Martigues. It flew low for 500 m and touched down perfectly. Later it made flights of more than 6 km. It was powered by the famous Gnome 50 hp, 7-cylinder radial engine.

The Curtiss flying boat of 1912. The central hull made an important contribution to this early model. It increased to a great extent the constructional possibilities of the machine.

The first thoroughbred aircraft, built for speed and highly advanced for its time, was the Deperdussin. Two Gnome engines in tandem developed 160 hp and drove it at 200 km an hour. This was in 1912. The seaplane version easily won the first Schneider Trophy which was competed for in 1913.

29

HIGHER AND FASTER

It seems that as soon as Blériot succeeded in crossing the Channel, men's ideas about aviation began to grow clearer. Technical improvements to aircraft began to proliferate, putting to an end, once and for all, guesswork, improvisation, and shoddiness.

Dazzled by the extraordinary flights of the Wright brothers, many pioneers and fans followed their building pattern. But it was soon clear that Blériot's plan of putting all the rudders at the rear of the aircraft was more efficient. Little by little, too, the practice of obtaining lateral control by means of warping the wing, was abandoned. Ailerons were used instead, and these allowed for greater sturdiness in the framework.

The biplane was preferred to the monoplane because of the greater feeling of security it provided on landing. Because of its low wing loading, it could fly very slowly without stalling. As a result, there grew up a strong prejudice against the monoplane, in spite of the latter's having proved to be very effective. Time alone would justify the champions of the monoplane, confirming its qualities by flights made by such sensational machines as the Antoinette, the Taube, The Fokker Spin, the Blériot itself, the Moranes, and especially the Deperdussin, that startling machine previously mentioned and seen below, the forerunner of specialized racing aircraft.

Did you know...

...that the name of the Taube monoplane was given to it because of its resemblance to a dove, and the word in German means just that?

In 1910 there appeared the above aeroplane that was the forerunner of today's jet aircraft. It was built by a Romanian called Henry Coanda. In place of a propeller it carried a turbine driven by a 50 hp Clerget engine. Its inventor had solved a number of significant problems but, for lack of power, it never actually flew.

In contrast, this flying wing on the right not only flew but flew very well. It was built by John Dunne (1875–1949), and on its maiden flight in 1910 it proved so stable that there was no need to touch the controls in level flight.

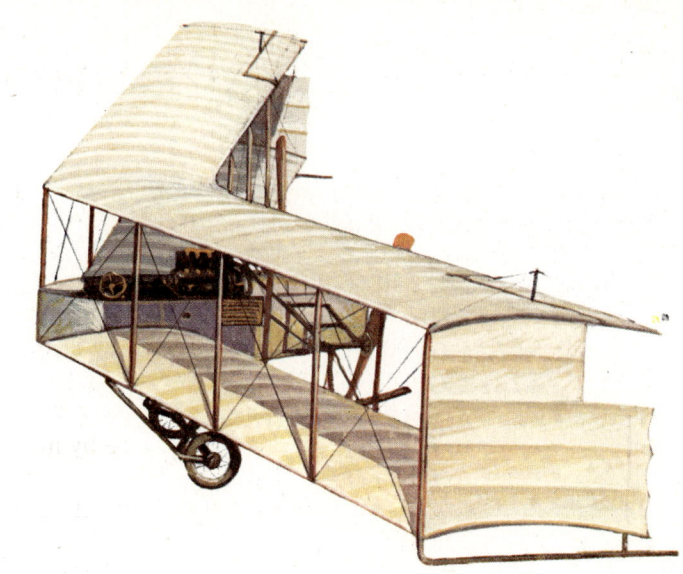

The first successful twin-engined machine was this Sommer of 1910. Like many others of its time, it was built on the Wright brothers' plan, just as they themselves had decided to abandon the forward elevator in their model of that year.

Above are two surprising aircraft, each for a different reason.
On the left is the Taube monoplane. Thanks to its powerful 100 hp Mercedes engine, this machine behaved very well, provided it wasn't asked to manoeuvre too violently. It was built by the Austrian engineer Igo Etrich, and 50 of them took part in World War I. On the right is the Antoinette Latham Monobloc of 1911. It was an extraordinary, highly advanced design which, on the face of it, looked destined for success. But it never actually got airborne. It seems incredible that such an experienced designer as Latham should fail to realize that a 50 hp engine just would not be capable of lifting a load of 1,350 kg. This notable lack of power ensured failure from the outset.

REFINEMENTS BEFORE WORLD WAR I

According to existing records, aviation was going ahead in Russia in the days of the Czar. In 1913 the Russians built and successfully flew the world's first four-engined aircraft. This was the *Russkii Vitiaz* (Russian Gentleman), an enormous machine designed by Igor Sikorsky and G.I. Lavrov. This aircraft was destroyed on the ground in a unique accident. A biplane in flight lost its engine, which plunged earthwards and landed precisely on top of the four-engined monster.

The Russians did not waste time trying to repair it. Instead, they built an even larger plane, the *Ilia Mourometz* (seen here). It had electric light, central heating, tables, chairs, and couches, a dining room, and an outside promenade deck where passengers could take a walk during the flight. It was test-flown at the end of 1913 and immediately demonstrated its capabilities. In 1914 it set up a number of records. It carried 16 passengers at a height of 2,000 m for five uninterrupted hours, and it was able to keep flying in a straight line on just two engines. Because of its great potential as a bomber, some time later in 1916 both the British and the French sought permission to manufacture it under licence. But they never did build it.

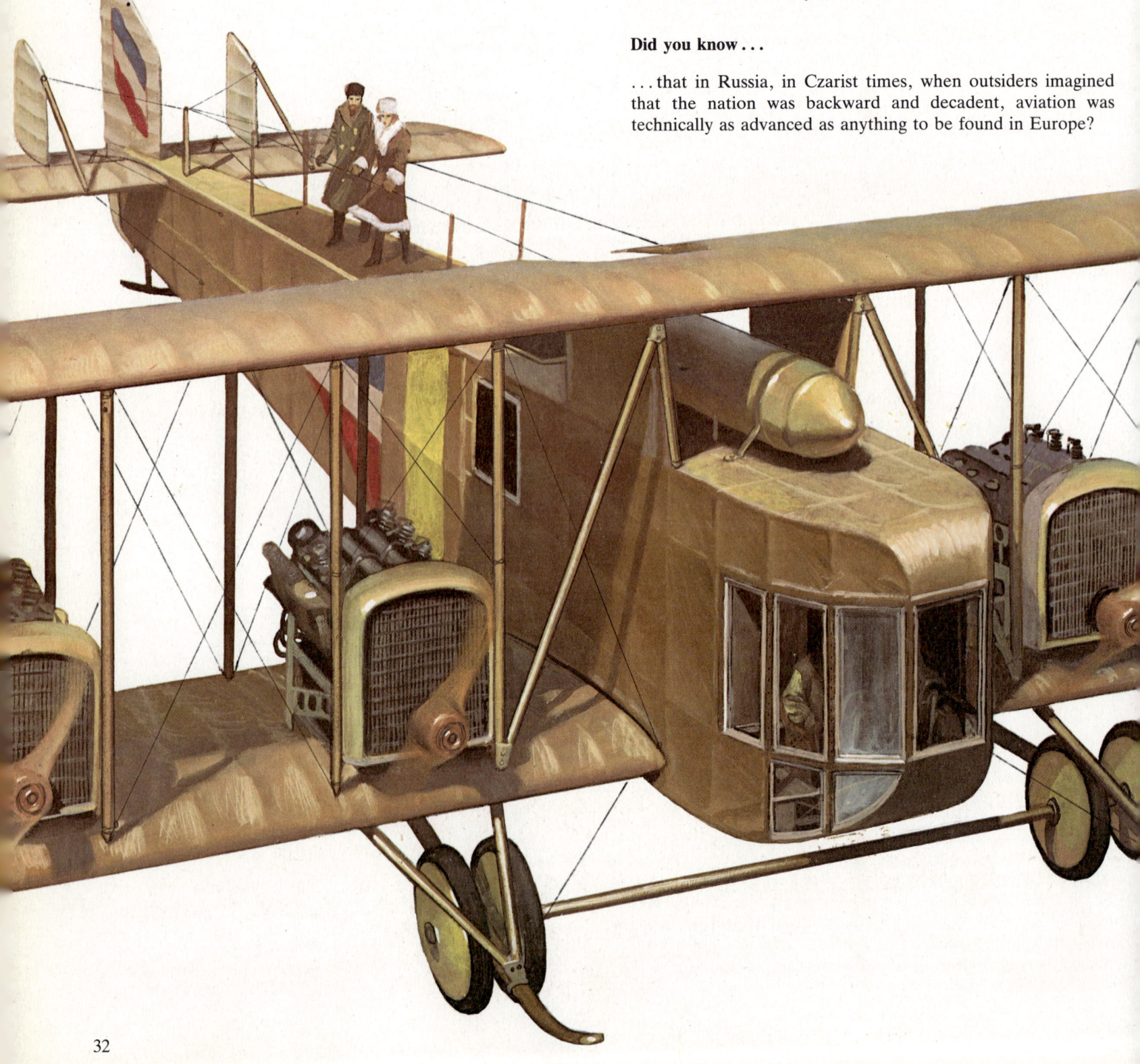

Did you know...

...that in Russia, in Czarist times, when outsiders imagined that the nation was backward and decadent, aviation was technically as advanced as anything to be found in Europe?

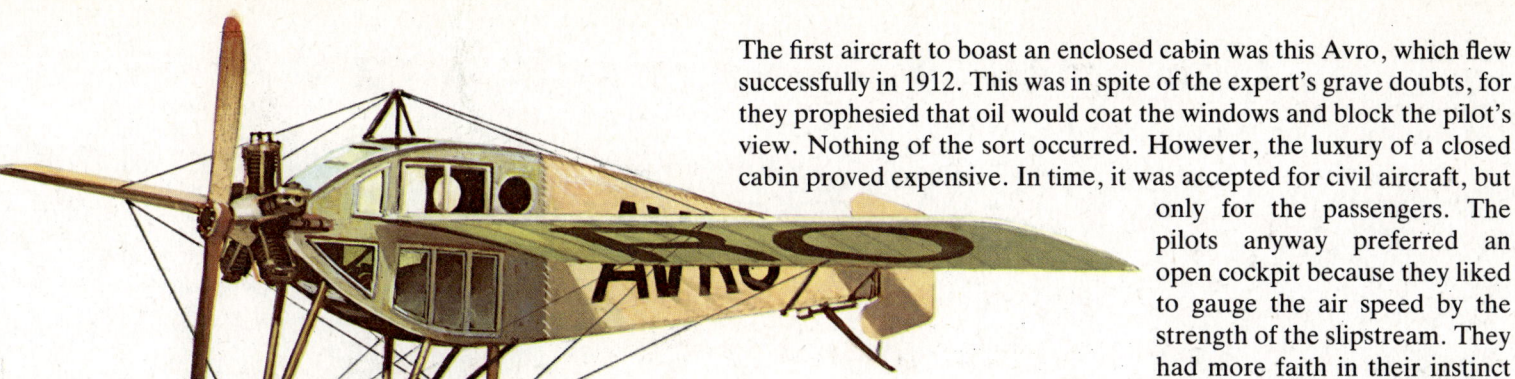

The first aircraft to boast an enclosed cabin was this Avro, which flew successfully in 1912. This was in spite of the expert's grave doubts, for they prophesied that oil would coat the windows and block the pilot's view. Nothing of the sort occurred. However, the luxury of a closed cabin proved expensive. In time, it was accepted for civil aircraft, but only for the passengers. The pilots anyway preferred an open cockpit because they liked to gauge the air speed by the strength of the slipstream. They had more faith in their instinct than in the primitive instruments.

Above is the Blériot XXI, which was displayed in the Great Palace exhibition of 1912. True to his monoplane convictions, Blériot with this model showed how much he had cleaned up the lines of the aircraft. At that time there was much debate over monoplane versus biplane.

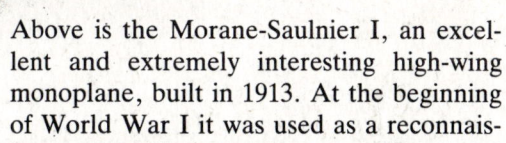

Above is the Morane-Saulnier I, an excellent and extremely interesting high-wing monoplane, built in 1913. At the beginning of World War I it was used as a reconnaissance plane, but because it flew so well it was later also employed as a fighter. This principle of using a single parasol wing was to prove its undoubted worth many years later.

The argument about the rival merits of one wing or two swung in favour of the latter with the appearance of the Sopwith Tabloid in 1913. This machine won the Schneider Trophy in 1914, in the absence of the Deperdussin. It flew at 140 km an hour and was used for reconnaissance in World War I.

The 1913 Avro 504, shown above, helped to restore the balance in favour of the biplane. It was so successful that more than 10,000 of them were built. Some of these were still flying in 1939. In World War I the Avro was used as reconnaissance aircraft and a light bomber.

This 1913 Henry Farman was a typical example of the machines that stuck to the Wright brothers' formula. Freed from forward obstacles, the pilot's cockpit became doubly important because a gun could be fired ahead without hindrance from a propeller. Later, when machine guns were synchronized with the prop blades, these machines disappeared as fighters and became obsolete as bombers as early as 1916.

THE FIRST AIRCRAFT OF WORLD WAR I

Quenault, the French mechanic airgunner, paled when, at the height of a dogfight against the German Aviatik his 7 mm Hotchkiss machine gun jammed. He was about to tell his pilot, Sergeant Frantz, about this awkward situation, when suddenly the Aviatik lifted its nose and fell into a spin. This happened on 5 October 1914 and is recorded as the first aircraft to be downed in World War I. The ill-equipped pilots possessed only one gun.

At the outbreak of war the generals found themselves with a new weapon to hand—the aeroplane. With some distrust, they decided to go ahead and use it. At first they used it for observation duties and also for artillery spotting. As a result, the sky was soon filled with 'spies', which relayed information back to their respective sides. At first these aircraft were unarmed and the rival pilots gave each other a formal salute when they met. But this state of affairs obviously could not last, and orders were changed. From then on all enemy aircraft encountered in flight were to be shot down. Rifles and pistols were immediately brought into use, but these weapons proved to be quite inneffectual, some because they were too slow-firing and others because of their limited range. It became obvious that the ideal weapon, in spite of its weight, was the machine gun.

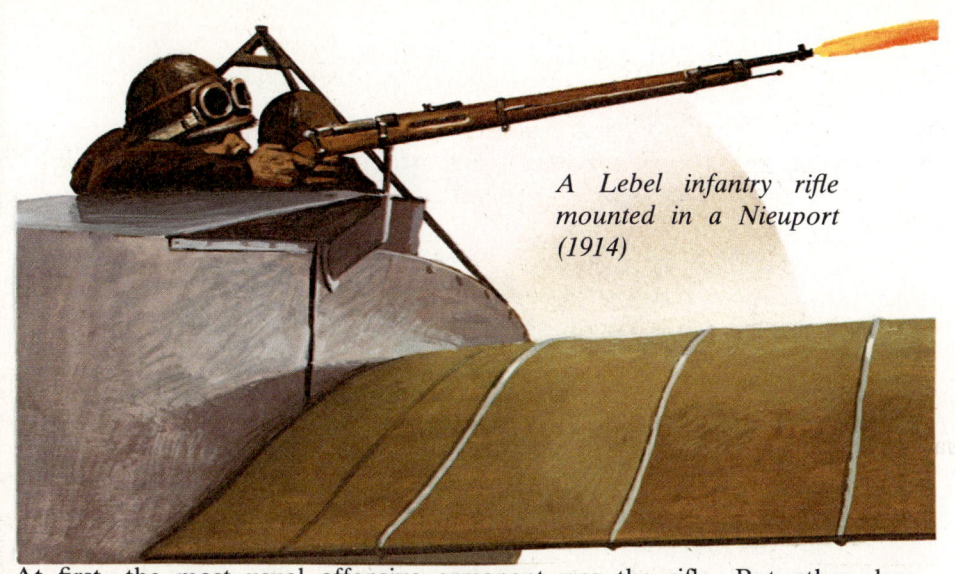

A Lebel infantry rifle mounted in a Nieuport (1914)

At first, the most usual offensive armament was the rifle. But other, less orthodox means were not overlooked. These included the use of hand grenades, shotguns, trailing anchors, and even the hurling of bricks. But they all proved more or less ineffectual.

Pilots were equipped with effective pistols. The weapons had to have either a good range, like the Mauser, or a large calibre, like the Colt. Shown here is one of the latter, of .45 calibre. It carried 20 bullets in the chamber and had a compartment into which the empty cartridge cases tumbled.

The Albatros B II was the most widely used of the German reconnaissance planes in the first year of the war. Its top speed was 105 km an hour and it could climb to 3,000 m. It was an unarmed two-seater.

One of the most important duties of the aeroplane was the bombing mission. In order to meet this requirement, the most likely looking aircraft on the market were soon recruited. This Caudron was one of the first to be thus used. It was an excellent choice.

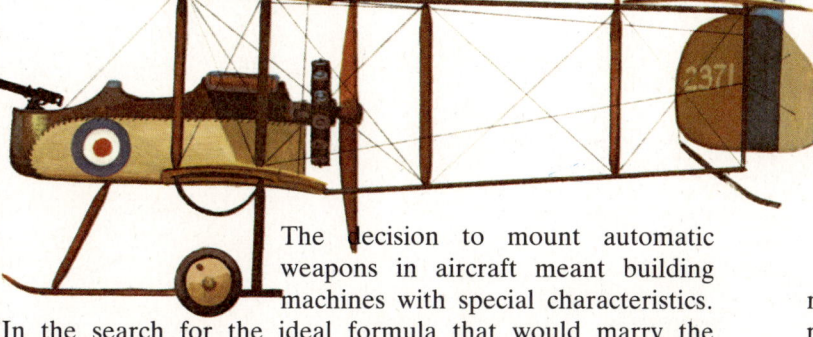

The decision to mount automatic weapons in aircraft meant building machines with special characteristics. In the search for the ideal formula that would marry the aeroplane and the machine gun, the British came up with this Vickers F.B.5, built specially for the use of a forward-firing gun.

The French gave this Nieuport Bebé a fixed machine gun in 1915. It was mounted centrally on the upper wing, clear of the radius of the propeller blades. The idea was to align the gun by aiming the whole aircraft at the target—a revolutionary method initiated by Roland Garros in 1905.

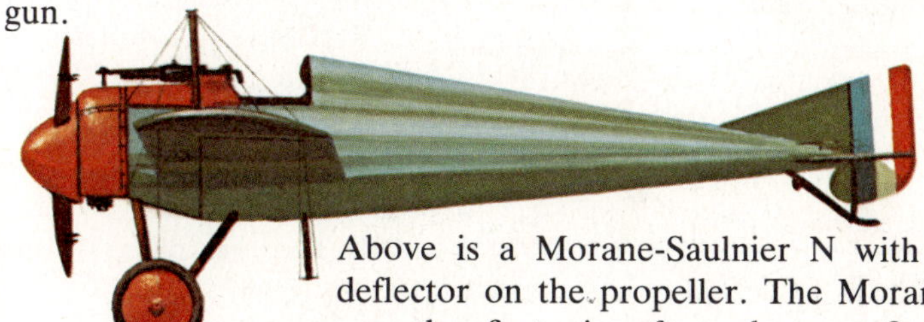

Above is a Morane-Saulnier N with a deflector on the propeller. The Morane was the first aircraft to have a fixed machine gun on the engine cowling. When the pilot wanted to attack, he pointed the whole aircraft at the target, and this brought a new dimension to air warfare. To stop the propeller's blades being torn to shreds by the bullets, the blades carried a steel deflector.

At last a true, no compromise fighter appeared on the scene. It was an ideal combination of aircraft, man, and machine gun. With its gun synchronized with the propeller, this Fokker E III played havoc with the Allied air fleets. It gave the Germans air supremacy for a whole year, until the Allies built similar aircraft.

The Handley Page 0/400

THE BOMBERS

At the beginning of World War I—which was initially seen as an artillery duel—hardly anyone in the higher echelons had any faith in aerial bombardment. The most they would concede was that airships might be useful for a few long-range attacks. Time was to show how mistaken these people were, for in September 1914 the British, using Avro 504s, carried out a strategic raid on the German Zeppelin factory and hangars.

On the other hand, forecasts about the Zeppelin's role in air warfare were borne out when, early in 1915, the Germans used them to launch a series of air attacks on London. The damage was slight, but what disturbed public opinion more was the fact that defence measures against the airships were completely useless, especially when they flew by night.

In 1916 the Allies began to use the Buckingham incendiary bullet, and this was a death blow to the highly vulnerable German airships, forcing them to retreat from the battle line. But the Germans refused to be discouraged and produced out of the hat, as it were, a true strategic long-range bomber, the huge Gotha, which could carry a heavy bomb load.

Meanwhile the British concentrated on aircraft design, especially the bomber, and came up with the famous Handley Page. By the end of the war, the bomber was already well developed. There were basically three kinds of bombers: light, medium, and heavy.

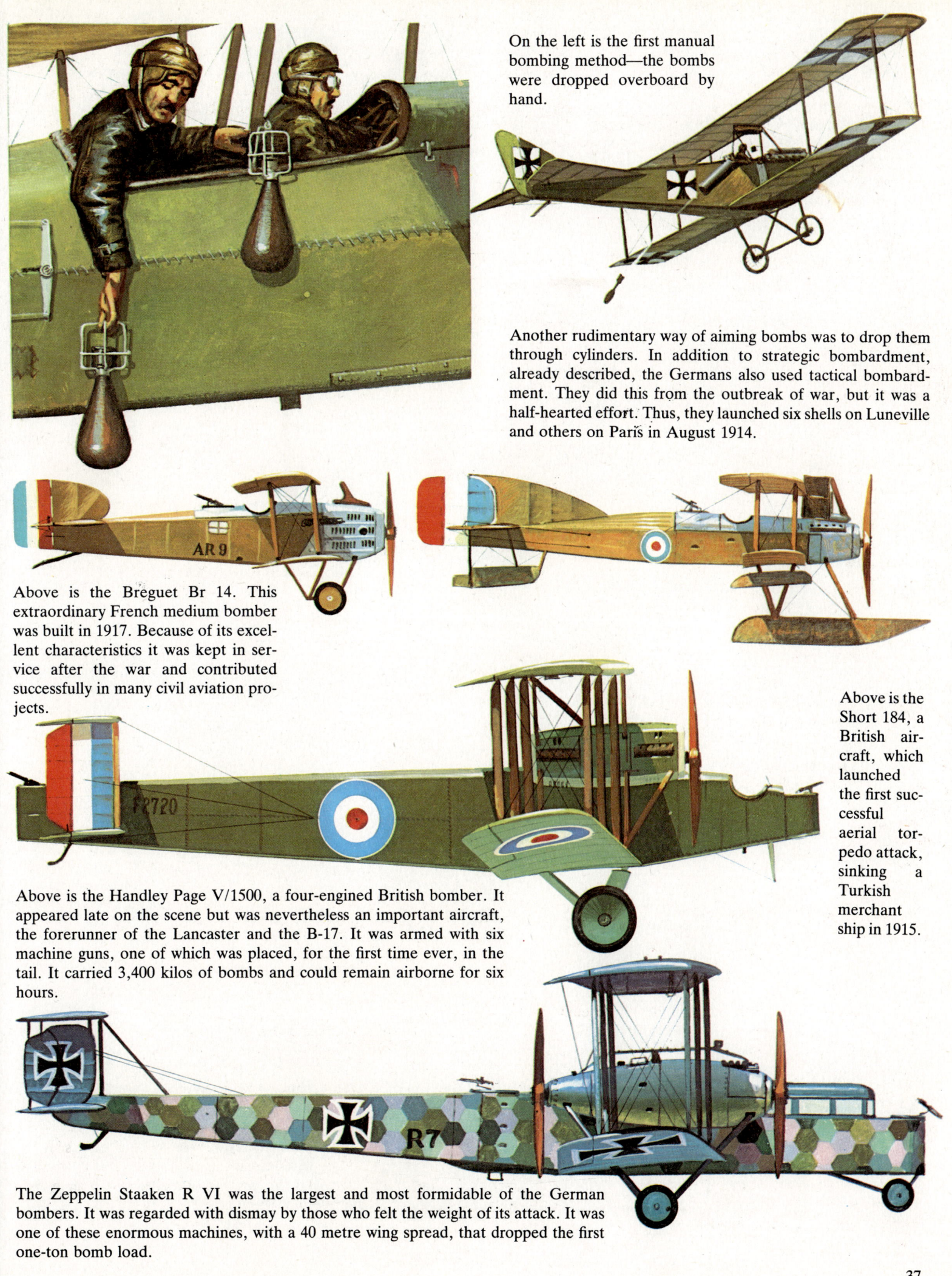

On the left is the first manual bombing method—the bombs were dropped overboard by hand.

Another rudimentary way of aiming bombs was to drop them through cylinders. In addition to strategic bombardment, already described, the Germans also used tactical bombardment. They did this from the outbreak of war, but it was a half-hearted effort. Thus, they launched six shells on Luneville and others on Paris in August 1914.

Above is the Breguet Br 14. This extraordinary French medium bomber was built in 1917. Because of its excellent characteristics it was kept in service after the war and contributed successfully in many civil aviation projects.

Above is the Short 184, a British aircraft, which launched the first successful aerial torpedo attack, sinking a Turkish merchant ship in 1915.

Above is the Handley Page V/1500, a four-engined British bomber. It appeared late on the scene but was nevertheless an important aircraft, the forerunner of the Lancaster and the B-17. It was armed with six machine guns, one of which was placed, for the first time ever, in the tail. It carried 3,400 kilos of bombs and could remain airborne for six hours.

The Zeppelin Staaken R VI was the largest and most formidable of the German bombers. It was regarded with dismay by those who felt the weight of its attack. It was one of these enormous machines, with a 40 metre wing spread, that dropped the first one-ton bomb load.

A NEW BREED OF FIGHTERS

'Then I slowly pulled back on the stick and gained a little height—a rule in air warfare. Now... I raked the whole side of the enemy plane with a burst of machine-gun fire. The pilot turned his head and looked at me. I could see his eyes gleaming behind the big goggles. Then, as the bullets thudded all round him, he slumped in his seat. He had stopped firing. Richthofen was dead. Everything happened in a matter of seconds: it took much less time than it takes to tell it. His plane wobbled, went into a dive, and hit the deck.'

(From the account by Canadian pilot, Captain A. R. Brown of his aerial dogfight with Baron von Richthofen [1892–1918].)

This is the French Nieuport 17, evolved from the Bébé of 1914, and regarded as one of the finest fighter aircraft of its time. It was the favourite aircraft of such aces as the Englishman Ball, Canadian Bishop and the Frenchmen Nungesser, Guynemer, Fonck, and Navarre.

The performance of this machine greatly worried the Germans, and they finally decided to copy it. But they never actually got round to it because of the advent of a powerful version of the Albatros.

The French SPAD VII was said to be unquestionably the very best fighter of the first half of the war. It was built by Louis Bechereau, the originator of the unforgettable Deperdussin, although much of the machine's success was due to its engine, a V8, 150 hp Hispano-Suiza, designed by the astonishing Swiss engineer Marc Birkigt. The perfecting of these new in-line engines spelled intense competition for the older radial types.

This is one of the RAF's SE 5As, one of the better British fighters. Tough, manoeuvrable, and extremely fast, it showed itself superior to both the Albatros D III and the Fokker Dr I. It first appeared in 1917 and it made a decisive contribution to the Allies' regaining of air superiority in the last years of the war.

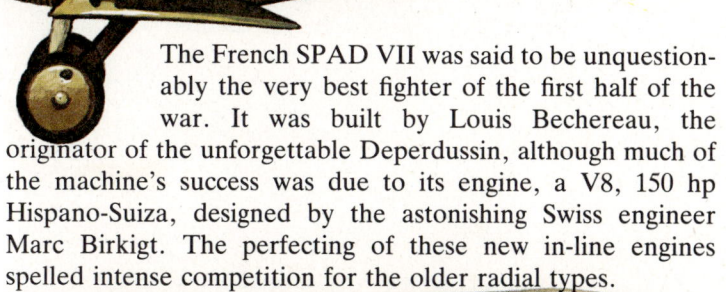

The Sopwith 2F1 Camel was a temperamental fighter which was difficult to control because of the powerful gyroscopic effect produced by its 130 hp rotary engine. This engine caused unpredictable shifts in equilibrium in the turns, although in expert hands the aircraft was surprisingly manoeuvrable, ideal for short-range combat. It was better than any other machine, except perhaps the Fokker triplane.

The Junkers D 1, seen above, was a 1918 German fighter with an excellent performance. It was unusual in being an all metal machine, covered with a hardened corrugated aluminium surface, typical of the Junkers factory from 1915 until the early 1930s. Note also the advanced design, which seems to belong to a much later period.

This is the Bristol M1C of 1917. Here was a clear example of how prejudice can affect vital decisions. In spite of demonstrating in trials that it was highly manoeuvrable and extremely fast (it achieved a speed of 212 km an hour with an engine of barely 110 hp) it was eventually turned down because it was a monoplane.

The Fokker D VII was unanimously regarded as the best German fighter and perhaps the best in the skies. It was Germany's last desperate attempt to achieve mastery of the air. It was tough, fast, and manoeuvrable, with a high rate of climb. Above all, it had great power at high altitudes, thanks to its 6-cylinder in-line Mercedes D III engine of 160 hp. One of the armistice clauses expressly required Germany to hand over the Fokker D VII to the victorious Allies as part of the spoils of war.

THE IMMEDIATE POST-WAR YEARS

With the end of World War I a new era began. The Treaty of Versailles appeared to ensure a long reign of peace, and the soldiers returned to their homes. But going home after nearly five years absence could present problems, especially for the young men who found themselves without a trade or profession and faced with the necessity of finding a job. The airmen found themselves in a similar position for, although they had learnt to fly, there was really no call for their services. Many of them refused to give up flying—a predilection that had originally driven them to volunteer for their respective air forces. Now, in peacetime, the air forces had all been drastically reduced. Apart from the aircraft industry itself, which had grown substantially thanks to the war, there was almost no chance of finding a job as a military pilot, and the small civil aircraft side had been even further reduced because of the war.

As things were, a number of pilots found jobs where they could in civil flying or sought fame and fortune in long-distance pioneer flights.

Did you know...

...that because of the shortage of jobs some pilots turned to aerobatics at risk of life and limb, or to making hair-raising flights for the silent films, to the thrill and delight of the movie fans of those days?

The feats of some of the post-war pilots electrified the public. In 1919, Védrines landed on the roof of the Lafayette Galleries, and Godefroy flew through the Arc de Triomphe in his Nieuport on the left.

The carrying of mail by air had been started before the war, but after the war, with much improved aircraft, the service became a regular one and many pilots found a niche delivering airmail as above.

Some of the outstanding bombers were rescued and pressed into civilian service. After reconditioning, they gave sterling performances. For example, the first non-stop crossing of the Atlantic was carried out in 1919 by the British airmen John Alcock (1892–1919) and Arthur Brown (1886–1948) in a Vickers Vimy. They used the bomb bay to store extra fuel.

This is the Farman Goliath, a plane which was originally designed as a bomber in 1918. Nevertheless, it later became famous as a passenger aircraft. It operated on scheduled air routes until 1933. In 1919 it was used by the French to inaugurate their international services.

CIVIL AVIATION IN THE 1920s

Pre-war commercial flying had been carried out by airships because the aircraft of the era were not considered reliable enough. But the great technical evolution sparked off by World War I transformed aeroplanes into something safe enough to attract an eager public and make commercial aviation profitable. It was at this point that a number of scheduled airlines, subsidized by their respective governments, began to make their appearance.

Also in Europe, the aircraft industry began to be revitalized, although at first rather timidly, after its rundown over the previous years. New aircraft, designed and built exclusively for civil duties, began to take to the air. This led to a significant expansion of the civil aircraft industry at the expense of military planes, which lagged seriously behind. This state of affairs lasted almost until the outbreak of World War II.

The picture shows a three-engined Ford, which first flew in 1925. This machine, designed on the lines of the famous Fokker, was the first American contribution to the world of civil aviation. Nicknamed the 'Tin Goose', it was bought by more than 100 aviation companies throughout the world and became a legend in its own time.

Did you know...

...that in February 1919 the Germans were the first to inaugurate a direct intercity air link (between Berlin and Weimar) using AEG J 11 aircraft, which were converted warplanes?

This is the Airco (de Havilland) D.H.4 converted for the carrying of passengers. It was one of the first aircraft to be used in peacetime and was employed by various companies. In December 1919 it broke the speed record from Paris to London, flying the distance in 1 hour 48 minutes, with two passengers up.

The Junkers F 13 made a really exceptional contribution to the development of civil aviation. Much of its success was due to its durability. It was built in the typical Junkers tradition, having an all-metal framework covered with corrugated metal-skinning. More than 300 of these were built, and some of them were still flying in 1938. They began to be turned out in 1919, and at that time their design was highly advanced.

Above is one of the first aircraft designed specifically for the civil market. It was the Blériot SPAD (1921). Not many were built, in spite of its success. The layout of the accommodation shows how uncertain the designers were in their search for the ideal.

The Dutch Fokker F II was their first for the civil air market. The prototype was built in Germany and, after many difficulties caused by export restrictions, it was presented to KLM, who accepted it enthusiastically in 1920. Later, Fokker produced 30 of these models, all of which gained great renown. These machines formed the first air link between Holland and Britain.

Unquestionably the most famous of the Fokkers was the F VIIb/3m on the right, a three-engined aircraft with outstanding characteristics. It was manufactured under licence in many countries, including Poland, Belgium, and Britain. It was also built in the United States, where Fokker had their own factory. Within a few years this machine was found in all parts of the world, operated by the principal airlines. It dates from 1928, and its cruising speed was nearly 200 km per hour.

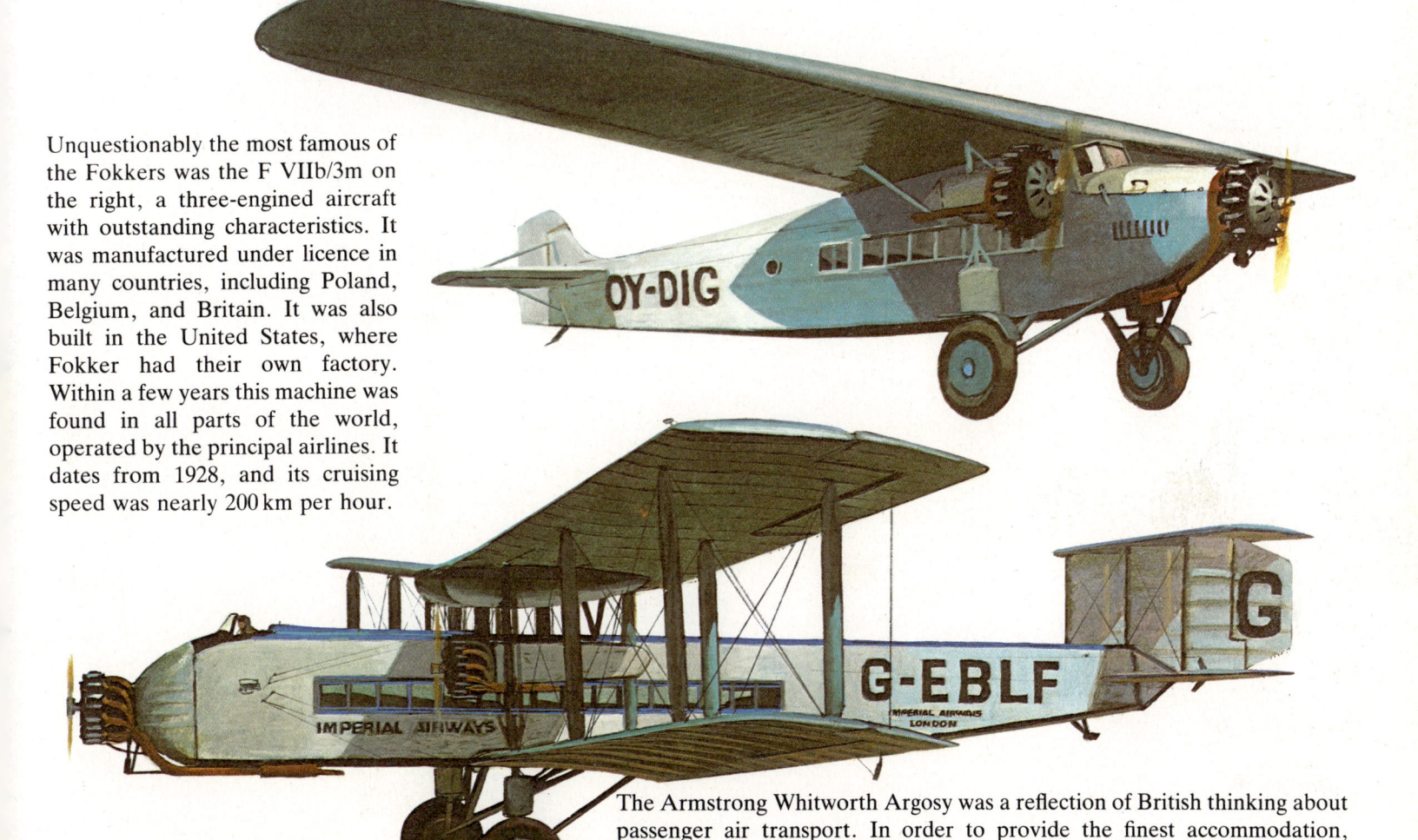

The Armstrong Whitworth Argosy was a reflection of British thinking about passenger air transport. In order to provide the finest accommodation, service, and safety, the British stuck to traditional constructional formulae, although these were somewhat antiquated, as can be clearly seen in this 1926 version.

WAR PLANES TO 1930

After World War I, the world's air forces were drastically reduced, and for some years military aircraft were distinguished neither for their brilliance nor for their technical improvements.

The typical military mentality at that time, sustained by the belief in a lasting peace, was unwilling to take risks in advanced designs, although these were powered by rapidly developing engines.

When civil aviation came up with some worthwhile technical improvement, the military duly adopted it. Nevertheless a few military brains were able to foresee that the aeroplane could be transformed into a formidable weapon. Among these far-sighted men was the American Billy Mitchell (1879–1936) who showed how effective a bomber could be against warships. As a result of which he was court-martialled.

In spite of the significant advances made by civil aircraft, there were some military pilots who succeeded in breaking a number of air-speed records.

The picture shows the first successful refuelling in flight, in 1923, by American aviators using de Havilland D.H.4s.

The Gloster Gamecock was a 1925 British fighter. The first post-war machines were clearly merely an extension of those that had finished the war. At this time the fixed radial engine was enjoying great popularity, after having been originally displaced by the rotary radial.

Another British fighter was this 1929 Bristol Bulldog. It was a good example of the second generation of fighters. It differed from its predecessors only in comparatively minor respects. The Bulldog proved to be a highly successful machine, fast, powerful, and extremely manoeuvrable. Its 490 hp engine gave it a top speed of 280 km per hour.

The growing importance of the radial engine led to a deep split between its supporters and those who defended the in-line engine. Above is the 1926 Fiat CR.20, a classic example of the in-line engined fighter. It boasted a V12 Fiat engine of 400 hp.

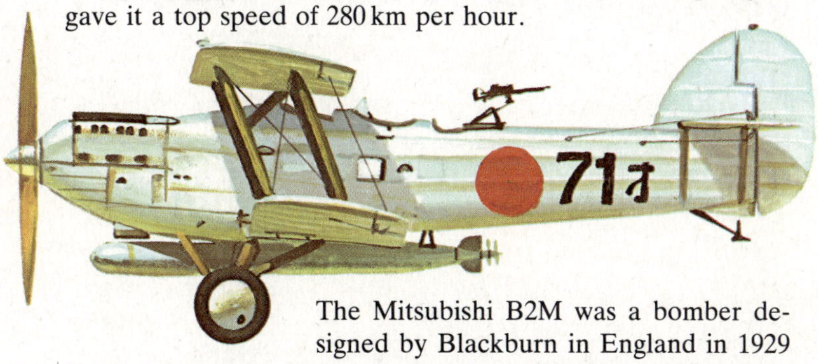

The Mitsubishi B2M was a bomber designed by Blackburn in England in 1929 for the Japanese. It was designed specifically as a torpedo-bomber. In order to be able to rival the technical expertise of the Europeans and Americans, the Japanese did not hesitate to entice foreign designers or order prototypes from them.

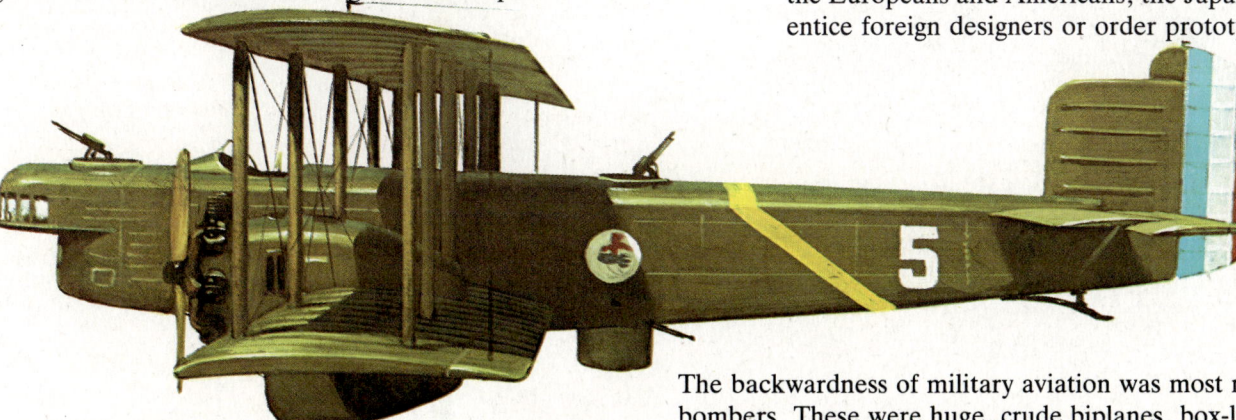

The backwardness of military aviation was most noticeable in the heavy bombers. These were huge, crude biplanes, box-like and slow, in an era when the monoplane had already demonstrated its paces.

At this time there took place two important events in the history of aviation. In 1923 the Spanish engineer Juan de la Cierva (1895–1936) began his first experiments with autogyros and laid the foundations for the development of the helicopter.

In 1928 the German Fritz Stamer piloted the world's first rocket-driven aircraft. It consisted of a Canard-type glider powered by rockets with powdered solid fuel. The project was partly financed by von Opel, the German car manufacturer. He also financed and flew the Opel-Sander Rak, another glider which, after several tests, flew for a hair-raising 1,500 m. These were the forerunners of the rocket fighters of World War II.

WAR PLANES: 1930–35

At the beginning of the 1930s, there was a great surge of reformatory zeal in military aviation circles, although the reforms were still rather timid. As a result, many new machines were highly advanced technically, while others retained their obsolete nature. Among civil aircraft, on the other hand, there were models that exhibited most of the refinements of modern planes. The 1931 Lockheed Orion, for example, was a low-wing cantilever monoplane with retractable undercarriage and enclosed cabin. Most military designers chose to incorporate only one or other of these innovations, as shown on the facing page. Perhaps the blame should really be laid at the door of the designers who, having been given the specifications for a new model, and knowing the prejudices of their customers, did not dare come up with too revolutionary ideas. Only if a manufacturer were to build an outstanding aircraft at his own expense would the customer then consider buying it. The following true story illustrates this attitude.

General Udet, German air ace of World War I and head of the technical division of Hitler's Luftwaffe, made a close examination in early 1935 of the new Bf 109, which at that time was just being built. He sat down in the enclosed cockpit and when he emerged he gave the inventor a friendly slap on the back. 'This will never be any good as a fighter, Messerschmitt,' he said. 'The pilot must have an open cockpit in order to gauge the airspeed by the strength of the slipstream. It really needs another wing above and a number of struts and wires. Then you'll have a real fighter. Eventually, after having put the plane through its paces, the General became enthusiastic, although Messerschmitt never quite lost his feeling of disgust over the incident.

At the beginning of the decade, with significant modifications being made to the radial engine, the performance and shape of aircraft gradually began to alter, as can be seen from this Boeing F4B-4.

The Hawker Fury I, a fine aircraft with elegant lines, was the ancestor of the famous British Hurricane. It first flew in 1931 and immediately impressed observers by the way it flew, but above all by its speed and its rate of climb at altitude. Its top speed was 333 km/h.

The Boeing P-26 was a famous American fighter of 1933, known as 'The Peashooter'. It was the first monoplane to be used by the US Army Air Corps. However, in spite of being a monoplane it had plenty of bracing wires and a fixed undercarriage. Boeing already had the B-9 bomber in service with retractable undercarriage.

The Morane-Saulnier 225 was an outstanding French fighter dating from 1932. True to the marque's tradition, it was a parasol-winged monoplane. It had the same attributes as the Hawker Fury, but boasted a smaller engine—a 9-cylinder Gnôme-Rhône radial engine of 500 hp. It had excellent manoeuvrability, and was chosen for various aerobatic displays. In 1935 it set a new altitude record of 9,791 m.

The Dewoitine D 510 was a notable French fighter that first flew in 1934. It immediately went into full production, and altogether 308 of these machines were built. It was the first French aircraft to reach 400 km/h in level flight. The 1934 version was the best armed fighter of that period. It carried a 20 mm Hispano automatic cannon that fired through the propeller hub, as well as the two obligatory machine guns.

The Grumman F3F was an American carrier-borne fighter that first flew in 1935. The US Navy regarded it as the finest aircraft in its class, which shows us how far US aviation lagged behind that of the other great powers in those days. This became painfully apparent in World War II when American aircraft first met their Japanese counterparts. The F3F was the predecessor of the Wildcat and of the later famous Hellcat.

The Polikarpov I-16 was a Russian fighter whose official debut in 1935 should have caused a sensation. At a time when the other major powers were still squeezing the last ounce of performance out of the biplane, this almost futuristic model should have astonished observers. It was unquestionably the most modern fighter of its time and first saw action in the Spanish Civil War.

CIVIL AVIATION TO 1935

At the beginning of the 1930s, once the civil airlines had established and consolidated themselves with an indoctrinated public, commercial competition waxed fierce to attract fare-paying customers. The companies owning the air fleets kept up a continuous pressure on the manfacturers to provide greater comfort, space, speed, and safety. As a result, the airliner evolved rapidly. Major steps towards the ideal were realized in 1933 with the appearance of the Boeing 247. In the meantime, experiments were being carried out which would determine the future of the commercial airliner. The only question that remained was, who would be the first to reap the benefit?

On the other hand, the airline companies felt that they must use flying boats on their ocean routes. As a result, the flying boat entered into a period of substantial expansion.

The picture shows a Sikorsky 43 amphibious flying boat taking off from the water. In spite of the fact that it was built in 1934 it has an undoubtedly modern look about it.

Did you know...

...that the French even transformed an elegant Lioré et Olivier into a flying restaurant, named 'The Golden Flash', which served the most delicious food?

Here are a few examples of the trends we have been discussing.

This is a 1931 Handley Page. True to their policies, the British preferred slow, majestic, safe machines with excellent in-flight service on the important routes. As far as service was concerned, the French too, took great pains to look after their passengers.

On the left is an Atalanta of 1932, carrying 17 passengers. This formula, which embodied four engines set in a high wing, with fixed undercarriage, was a popular one. The lines of the fuselage showed great aerodynamic improvement.

This is the well-known German Junkers Ju 52/3m. This was a typical product of that factory, whose airframes displayed distinct advantages over those of other machines. It dates from 1932 and the modern-looking fuselage should come as no surprise because Junkers were noted for their advanced designs.

Here is the Curtiss Condor of 1933, the aerodynamically clean lines of which display some similarity to those of the DC-2, pictured later on. The major difference is the retention of old-fashioned-looking biplane wings.

Below is the Martin M-130, known as the 'China Clipper'. It was one of the largest piston-engined planes of its era. We shall be discussing a few more giants of the air later on. This enormous flying boat, with its 40 m wingspan, flew for the first time in 1935. It was made to the order of Pan American, who specified a flying boat that could cover 6,000 km for the route from San Francisco to Manila, with stages at Honolulu, Midway, and Wake Island. There is no doubt that with the advent of this machine aviation was making new advances.

49

GIANTS OF THE AIRWAYS

The building of a huge passenger aircraft that would cover long distances, that would compete commercially with ships and trains, that would provide maximum comfort and still be a viable proposition, was a challenge that many manufacturers could not resist.

Some enormous aircraft, such as the Caproni, failed to take off properly. But others, such as the flying boats, achieved success. Either way, constructional difficulties, tremendous expense, and other technical problems resulted in relatively few of these craft being built. Later, the rapid development of land planes and the proliferation of airports tended to bypass the progress of the flying boat.

The picture shows the Latécoère 521, a French flying boat that was really the Jumbo of the 1930s. It had a wingspan of nearly 50 m and was 31 m long. It made its maiden flight in 1935 and set up a host of records. At take-off it weighed 38 tonnes and had a speed of 210 km per hour. Its maximum range was 4,100 km.

Above is the Caproni 60, an aerial 'train'. It was an ambitious project initiated in 1921 by the builder of a series of efficient bombers in World War I. But this craft was a complete failure because it could rise no more than a few metres into the air, and finally plunged into the waters of Lake Maggiore. It was built to carry 100 passengers across the Atlantic, but its lack of power and sheer impracticability ensured failure from the outset.

Another ill-starred giant was the Dornier Do X flying boat below, dating from 1929. It was powered by 12 Curtiss 600 hp engines, but even these could not lift it more than 500 m off the water. In 1930 it made a 16-month exhibition flight round the world. But repeated setbacks and breakdowns showed just how fallible it was in operation.

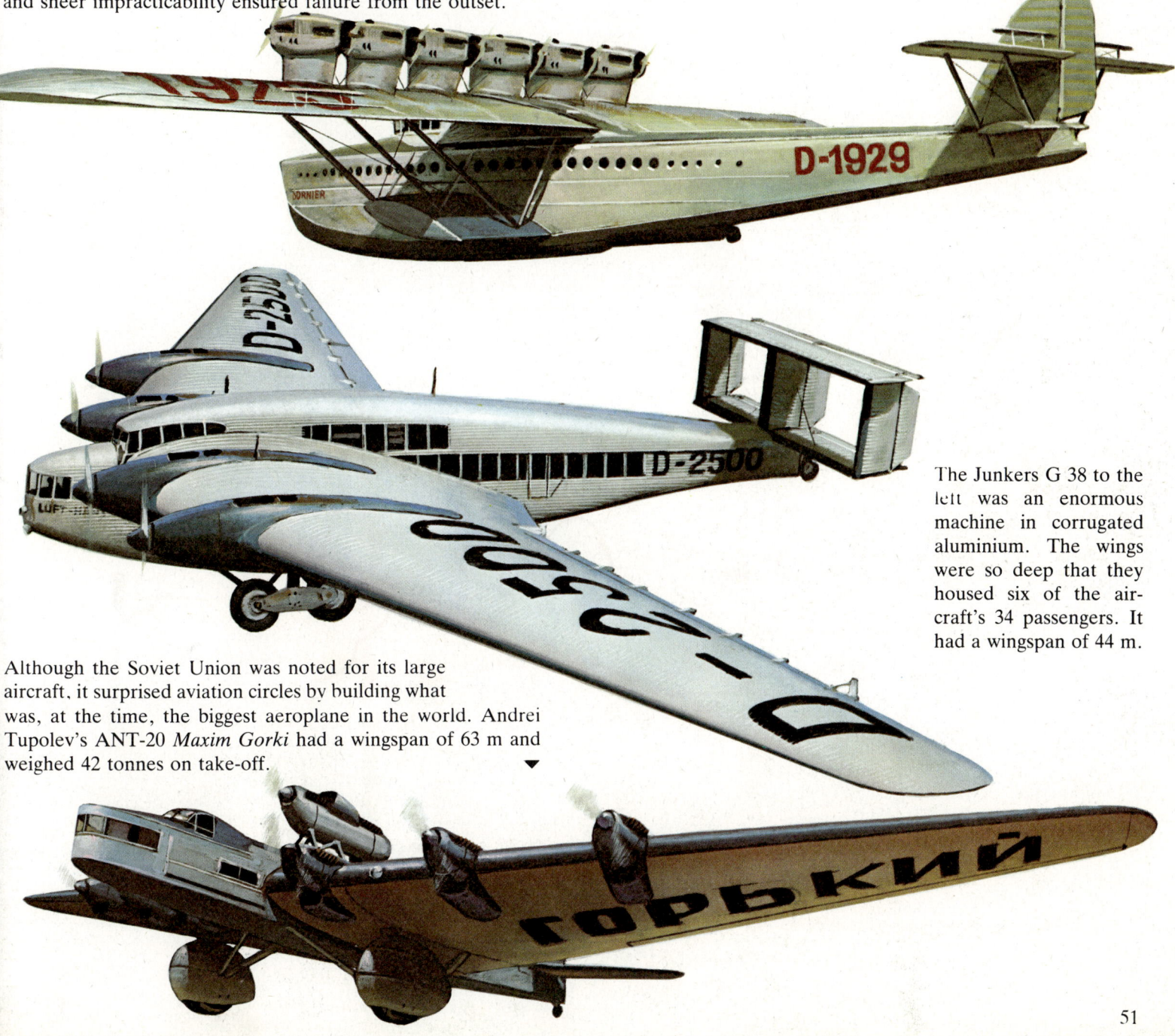

The Junkers G 38 to the left was an enormous machine in corrugated aluminium. The wings were so deep that they housed six of the aircraft's 34 passengers. It had a wingspan of 44 m.

Although the Soviet Union was noted for its large aircraft, it surprised aviation circles by building what was, at the time, the biggest aeroplane in the world. Andrei Tupolev's ANT-20 *Maxim Gorki* had a wingspan of 63 m and weighed 42 tonnes on take-off.

FLYING FUEL TANKS

Right from the start, aircraft set out to beat previously established records because this enhanced not only the prestige of the pilot and the manufacturer but also that of the country to which both belonged. One of the records most zealously challenged was that of distance covered, whether in closed circuit, in a straight line, or on a geographical crossing. A new record meant substantial rewards in hard cash.

In order to set new figures for long-distance flying an aircraft had to be virtually a flying fuel tank. At first, any kind of plane with suitably modified fuel tanks was thought good enough provided there was no engine failure (something that happened rather frequently). Later, machines were built specifically for the task. These had an enormous wing surface area and engines that were only just powerful enough to get the aircraft off the ground and keep it aloft with the minimum fuel consumption. One of the most famous of these long-distance crossings was that of Charles Lindbergh (1902–74), the American aviator, who made the first non-stop single-engined solo flight across the Atlantic. His machine, the *Spirit of St Louis* pictured here, was a Ryan and it carried not a gram of unnecessary weight. He took off from New York on 20 May 1927 and after 33½ hours landed in Paris to a hero's welcome.

The facing page shows a number of the most important aircraft that had appeared by the middle of the 1930s.

One cannot but admire the outstanding courage of the pilots whose feats so thrilled an air-minded public. They were fully aware of the risks they ran, crossing enormous wastes with the ever present possibility of an accident. These pilots achieved great personal popularity, but few survived into old age. A typical example was that of the legendary Mermoz who was killed in 1936 at the controls of the Latécoère *Southern Cross* which disappeared without trace on its last regular flight to North America.

This Fokker T-2 monoplane made the first non-stop flight across the USA in 1923. It was piloted by Lieutenants John Macready and Oakley G. Kelly, and they covered 4,100 km at an average speed of 150 km/h.

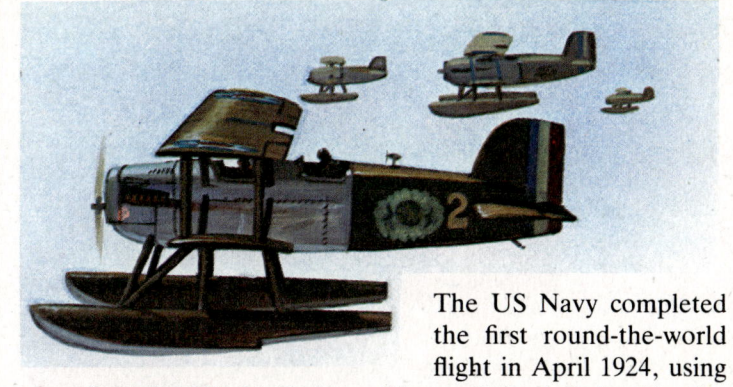

The US Navy completed the first round-the-world flight in April 1924, using four Douglas World Cruisers. They achieved their objective only after an accident-ridden journey lasting 175 days.

On 9 May 1926, the Americans Lt Cdr Richard Byrd and Floyd Bennett made the first flight over the North Pole, in a trimotor Fokker FVII/3m named *Josephine Ford*.

The Spaniard Ramón Franco crossed the South Atlantic in this Dornier Wal flying boat named *Plus Ultra*, setting up a new record for that type of machine.

The Italians established many new records, especially during the fascist era. This Savoia-Marchetti SM.64 achieved many world records. It was built in 1928 and it had a theoretical range of 11,500 km.

The first solo round-the-world flight was carried out by the American aviator Wiley Post (1900–35). He flew this Lockheed Vega *Winnie Mae* and did the trip in 115 hours 36 minutes. It was to remain unbeaten for more than 14 years.

France was one of the leading aeronautical nations and she enhanced her prestige with this Breguet 19, which made a number of epic flights. In 1930 it thrilled the public with the first east-west crossing of the North Atlantic from Paris to New York. The pilot was Capt. Dieudonné Coste.

This is the Tupolev ANT-25, which was specially commissioned by Josef Stalin. It had a theoretical range of 13,000 km. After smashing many records it achieved the world's longest flight in a straight line, from Moscow to San Jacinto in California, a distance of 10,075 km.

FASTER STILL: THE FLYING ENGINE

The designers of racing planes ideally aimed at building the lightest and smallest fuselage round the most powerful engine they could find. This was constant endeavour during the American air races of the 1930s. Speed competitions in which, naturally, records were regularly broken, date virtually from the beginning of true flight. As far back as 1909 there was the great aviation week held at Rheims. The Gordon Bennett trophy was also initiated. But it was in the United States that enthusiasm for air races reached its peak. As a result, many prizes were donated by commercial firms with an eye to publicity. Some of these became famous, among them Pulitzer, Thompson, Bendix, Lockheed, etc. There were also official trophies such as the National Air Races. In Europe the most prestigious event was the King's Cup Air Race, a British trophy. In the United States, speed competitions inspired small aero firms that specialized in racing planes, to take existing engines and then rebuild and specially tune them.

All in all, the scene was similar to today's Formula racing car set-up, or even more like the dragster scene. The aircraft shown here illustrates the point. It is the famous Gee Bee Wasp-engined R-1, which won the Thompson Trophy Race in 1931 and 1932, with speeds of 380 and 406 km an hour respectively. Although popular at the time, it was an ugly and difficult plane, and only gave of its best with an expert pilot at the controls. It was aimed purely at the speed fanatic. Such models were unquestionably dangerous, and they almost invariably crashed eventually, killing their pilots.

The Dayton-Wright RB Racer of 1920 was a competition machine that was built with the technical advice of Orville Wright to try for the Gordon Bennett trophy. It was a very fast plane of advanced design and was easily the most interesting entrant. It had to pull out of the race because of a broken cable, possibly sabotaged.

The Verville-Packard R-1 was a competition plane prepared by the US Army in 1920. It took part in the last of the Gordon Bennett races without success, but it won the first Pulitzer prize at an average speed of 251 km an hour. In a subsequent flight it touched 300 km/h.

This Curtiss-Cox racing plane was built in 1921 by the Curtiss Company for the oil magnate S. E. J. Cox. An excellent aircraft with triplane configuration to try and reduce landing speed, it confined its exploits to the Pulitzer competition. It was surprisingly beaten by the extraordinary Navy Curtiss CR-1, a seaplane version of which can be seen overleaf.

This is a clear example of what competition can do for aircraft design. This was a 1929 Verville-Sperry with a very modern silhouette. Its undercarriage was fully retractable. It failed to win the 1922 Pulitzer prize but it left the spectators gaping when the wheels disappeared.

On the left is the Travel Air Mystery Ship. This was the first plane to break the 200 mph (322 km/h) barrier and was the champion of the 1929 National Air Races. It owed its name to the secrecy that surrounded its trials, and its triumph to its 300 hp Wright engine, finely tuned to give 400 hp.

On the left is a good example of one of these elegant racing planes. This was a tiny machine called *Pete*, built by Ben Howard. It won the 1935 Bendix trophy.

The Wedell Williams on the left was an outstanding aircraft which won many competitions. Among these were the 1933 and 1934 Thompson trophies. It managed to clock 491 km an hour. It was often flown by Roscoe Turner, a great favourite with air racing fans and one who collected many prizes.

55

THE SCHNEIDER TROPHY

The Schneider Trophy was a coveted bronze sculpture offered by Frenchman Jacques Schneider to the Aero Club of France to be presented outright to the nation that won it three times consecutively or five times altogether. It was an annual competition reserved exclusively for seaplanes. Although originally intended to improve the quality of seaplanes, the competition later developed into a speed race round a closed circuit, carried out over the sea. The curious thing about this competition was that it became the most passionate and frenzied race of all, in which only the most advanced flying nations had any hope of succeeding and thus enhancing national prestige.

Poster advertising the Schneider Trophy

The Italians had always been good at building vehicles and engines for competition. They were not going to be outdone in aviation. The 1919 Schneider Trophy was anulled, although the Italians won a moral victory, and they were indisputable winners in 1920 and 1921. On the left is the 1921 victor, a Macchi M.7 *bis*. Its 280 hp Isotta-Fraschini engine drove it to a top speed of 257 km/h.

The 1922 race was won by a British Supermarine, which structurally resembled the Macchi. The rules governing the building of racing planes were changed in 1923. The winner this time was the Navy-Curtiss CR-3 on the left, the seaplane version of the exceptional CR-1. This aircraft reached a speed of 314 km/h with a 450 hp engine. This triumph decisively demonstrated to the world that the United States had overcome the wasted years of World War I.

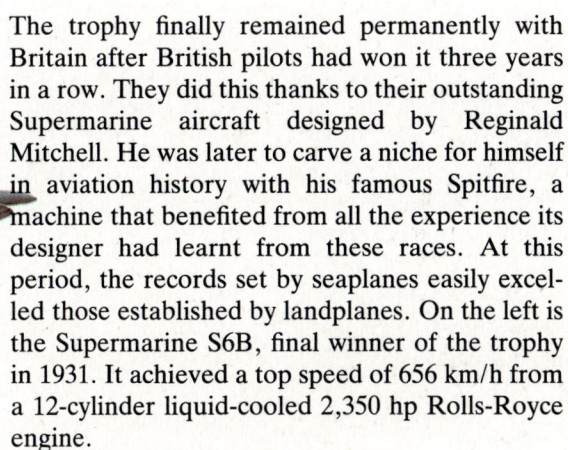

The trophy finally remained permanently with Britain after British pilots had won it three years in a row. They did this thanks to their outstanding Supermarine aircraft designed by Reginald Mitchell. He was later to carve a niche for himself in aviation history with his famous Spitfire, a machine that benefited from all the experience its designer had learnt from these races. At this period, the records set by seaplanes easily excelled those established by landplanes. On the left is the Supermarine S6B, final winner of the trophy in 1931. It achieved a top speed of 656 km/h from a 12-cylinder liquid-cooled 2,350 hp Rolls-Royce engine.

Had this Macchi-Castoldi MC.72 arrived in time for the last Schneider Trophy event, for which it had been designed and built, the British undoubtedly would not have won quite so easily. Nevertheless, this Italian seaplane passed into history as the last and finest of all the world's racing seaplanes. In 1934 it established a speed record for seaplanes that has never been beaten and most probably never will. With a top speed of 711 km/h when most of its fastest contemporaries could barely achieve 500 km/h, it could fairly lay claim to being the fastest piston-engined seaplane of all time. It owed this phenomenal performance unquestionably to its power plant, specially manufactured by Fiat. There were two V12 engines in tandem producing a total of 3,000 hp.

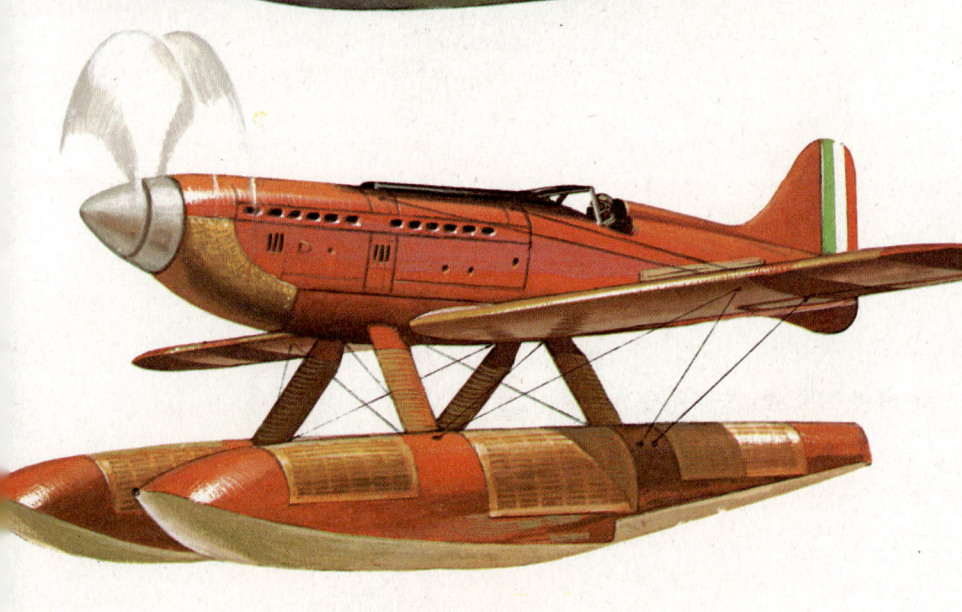

GETTING UP-TO-DATE

The Boeing 247, which first took to the air in February 1933, marked the beginning of an era. It was the first of a modern generation of airliners built of metal that were twin-engined, low-wing monoplanes with retractable undercarriage. They also incorporated other refinements such as variable-pitch propellers, flaps and elevators, automatic pilot, and de-icing equipment. With a cruising speed of 249 km/h and a maximum of 293 km/h, this Boeing was as fast as many fighters of that time in regular service.

United States Air Lines, which had a monopoly on this machine, immediately cornered the lion's share of the American market.

As a logical reply to this tough competition and also as a means of survival, Transworld Airlines then turned urgently to the Douglas Company, who came up with their DC-1, which flew for the first time in the middle of 1933.

The DC-1 not only matched the Boeing in most ways but also surpassed it in having room for four more passengers (the Boeing carried ten) in a more spacious and comfortable cabin.

Boeing 247

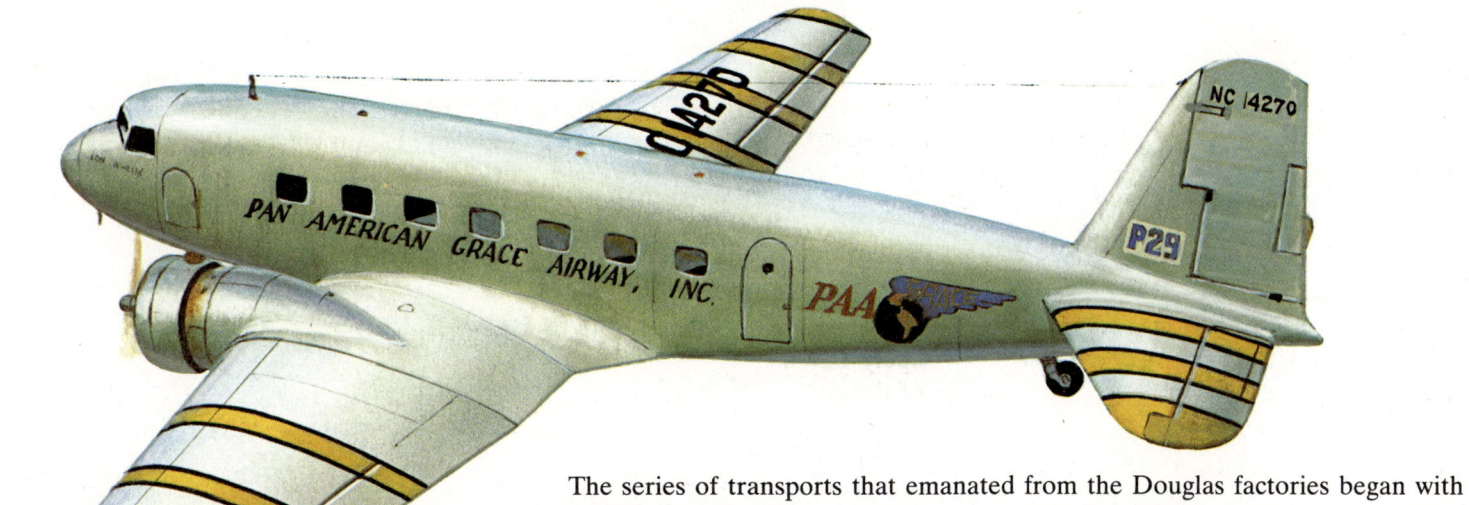

The series of transports that emanated from the Douglas factories began with the DC-2, seen above, an improved version of the DC-1. This first flew in May 1934, immediately beating the records set up by the Boeing 247. The aircraft was a huge success and Douglas received a flood of orders from rival firms.

The appearance in 1933 of these twin-engined machines from Boeing and Douglas tolled the knell of the earlier fast, luxurious single-engined airliners, not least for economic reasons—an important consideration in the years of the Depression. Boeing's success inspired rival firms to re-think and re-jig their designs.

The Vultee V-1A, seen above, was just such a victim. This machine was regarded in its day as the fastest and most advanced of the American light airliners. It dates from 1934.

Above is the Lockheed Electra, which flew for the first time in 1934. The industrialist who built it was renowned for his advanced ideas, for at that time an all-metal machine such as this was unheard of. In spite of its outstanding characteristics, the demand for this plane was nothing like that of the DC-2, although many later highly successful commercial light aircraft owed much to this design.

The DC-3 was the natural successor to the DC-2, and resulted from an order from American Airlines, who wanted a machine to take the place of their Curtiss Condors. The DC-3, shown below, which carried 14 to 32 passengers and was more powerful than its predecessor, was fabulously successful, far more so than the DC-2. All the American and most of the European airlines eventually bought the aircraft. It was such a sound machine that even today there are still many DC-3s left in service out of the 11,000 civil and military craft that were built.

CONCLUSION

This book closes at a crucial period in the history of aviation—at the birth of a further generation aeroplanes, which was the basis of all aeronautical construction and design, both civil and military, until jet aircraft began to take to the air.

The second volume covers the development of the aeroplane from the start of World War II until today. It deals with more than just aircraft, with a representative description of some of the personalities and events that influenced the progress of aviation. Together they add up to a fascinating historical survey specially prepared for the younger generation.

IMPORTANT DATES

1505 Leonardo da Vinci made the first detailed study in history of the dynamics of flight.

1766 English chemist Henry Cavendish discovered hydrogen; in those days it was called 'inflammable air'.

1782 French papermaker Joseph Montgolfier invented the hot air balloon.

1783 The brothers Joseph and Etienne Montgolfier made the first public ascent in a balloon on 4 June at Annonay in France.

1783 Jacques Charles and the Robert brothers launched the first hydrogen balloon on 28 August in Paris.

1783 The first animals (a rooster, a sheep, and a duck) ascended in a balloon over Versailles.

1783 Pilâtre de Rozier and the Marquis d'Arlandes became the first people to travel by air. They started off from La Muette gardens, near Paris, on 21 November.

1785 Jean-Pierre Blanchard and John Jeffries crossed the English Channel in a balloon on 7 January.

1794 On 2 June a captive balloon was used for military observation in the siege of Maubeuge.

1797 The first descent by parachute from the sky was carried out over Paris on 22 October by Frenchman André-Jacques Garnerin.

1804 On a scientific balloon ascent, French physicist Joseph Gay-Lussac reached a height of 7,016 m.

1808 The so-called father of aviation, British inventor Sir George Cayley tried out his first glider.

1842 Englishman William Henson patented his 'Aerial Steam Vehicle'.

1852 Frenchman Henri Giffard carried out the first motorized flight, between Paris and Trappes.

1871 At an exhibition in the Tuileries in Paris Alphonse Pénaud flew his *Planophore* a distance of 200 m.

1883 The Tisandier brothers successfully flew for the first time an airship driven by electricity.

1890 In his motorized machine *Eole*, Clément Ader was lifted a few centimetres off the ground over a distance of 50 m on 9 October.

1891 Otto Lillienthal carried out the first ever flight in a glider.

1900 Count Ferdinand von Zeppelin flew his first rigid airship across Lake Constance on 3 July.

1903 The Americans Orville and Wilbur Wright made the first true continuous flight in a motorized machine at Kitty Hawk, USA, on 17 December.

1904 On 3 August, Thomas Scott Baldwin's *California Arrow*, America's first airship, was tried out by Roy Knabenshue.

1906 Santos-Dumont carried out the first public aeroplane flight on 13 September at Bagatelle, Paris.

1909 On 25 July the French aviator Louis Blériot flew across the English Channel fron Calais to Dover.

1909 On 2 August the US Army officially adopted as its military aircraft a Wright machine.

1910 The first passenger service by Zeppelin was organized by the German firm of Delag.

1911 In July the US Navy adopted the Curtiss seaplane as its military aircraft.

1911 The first aerial crossing of the United States was undertaken by Galbraith P. Rodgers, linking New York with California. The journey lasted from 17 September to 10 December.

1911 Pierre Prior made the first nonstop flight from London to Paris on 12 April.

1917 The first giant German bombers appeared in the skies over London to replace the ill-fated Zeppelins.

1918 More than 1,500 Allied aircraft, under the command of General Billy Mitchell, carried out the first massive air raid in history against St Mihiel, in September.

1919 On 8 February the Farman Society inaugurated the first international air transport service, carrying passengers in a converted bomber from Paris to London.

1921 In February the first transcontinental air mail services were started in the United States. Planes flew both by day and by night.

1923 The first French national aviation company was founded, called Air Union; ten years later it was renamed Air France. The Belgians organized the Sabena company.

1924 Imperial Airways, the British aviation company, was founded.

1924 On 12 December the autogiro invented by the Spanish engineer Juan de la Cierva, was first tried out over a 12 km flight.

1925 The various German airlines were amalgamated and the Lufthansa company was founded.

1926 The Spanish flying boat *Plus Ultra*, commanded by Ramón Franco, flew from Palos to Buenos Aires from 22 January to 10 February: a distance of 10,270 km in 59 hours 39 minutes.

1926 On 9 May Commander Richard Byrd of the US Navy flew in a Fokker F VIIa/3m over the North Pole, piloted by Floyd Bennett.

1926 The first crossing by air of the north polar ice cap was carried out from 11 to 14 May. It was done in the airship *Norge*, which carried Roald Amundsen from Spitzberg to Alaska over the North Pole.

1927 The American aviator Charles Lindbergh crossed the Atlantic single-handed on a non-stop flight from New York to Paris on 20 and 21 May.

1927 Commander Byrd flew across the Atlantic with three companions non-stop in a trimotor Fokker, setting down in the surf off the Normandy coast because of poor visibility, on 1 July.

1929 On 28 November Commander Byrd flew over the South Pole in a trimotor Ford 4-AT-B.

1930 The French aviators Dieudonné Coste and Maurice Bellonte made the first non-stop flight from Paris to New York on 1 and 2 September.

1930 Two American airlines were founded: American Airways (25 January) and United Air Lines (30 June).

1931 On 26 May Swiss physicist Auguste Piccard became the first man to penetrate the stratosphere in an airtight gondola attached to a balloon, attaining a height of 15, 781 m.

1931 In June American aviators Wiley Post and Harold Gatty smashed all records for a round-the-world flight, achieving the feat in their Lockheed monoplanes in 8 days 15 hours and 51 minutes.

1931 On 29 August the German airship *Graf Zeppelin* inaugurated the first transatlantic air passenger service between Germany and Brazil.

1933 In July Wiley Post in his aircraft *Winnie Mae* flew round the world in 7¼ days, covering 24,954 km.

1936 The German airship *Hindenburg* made the first commercial scheduled transatlantic flight, from Frankfurt to Lakehurst, USA, on 6 May.

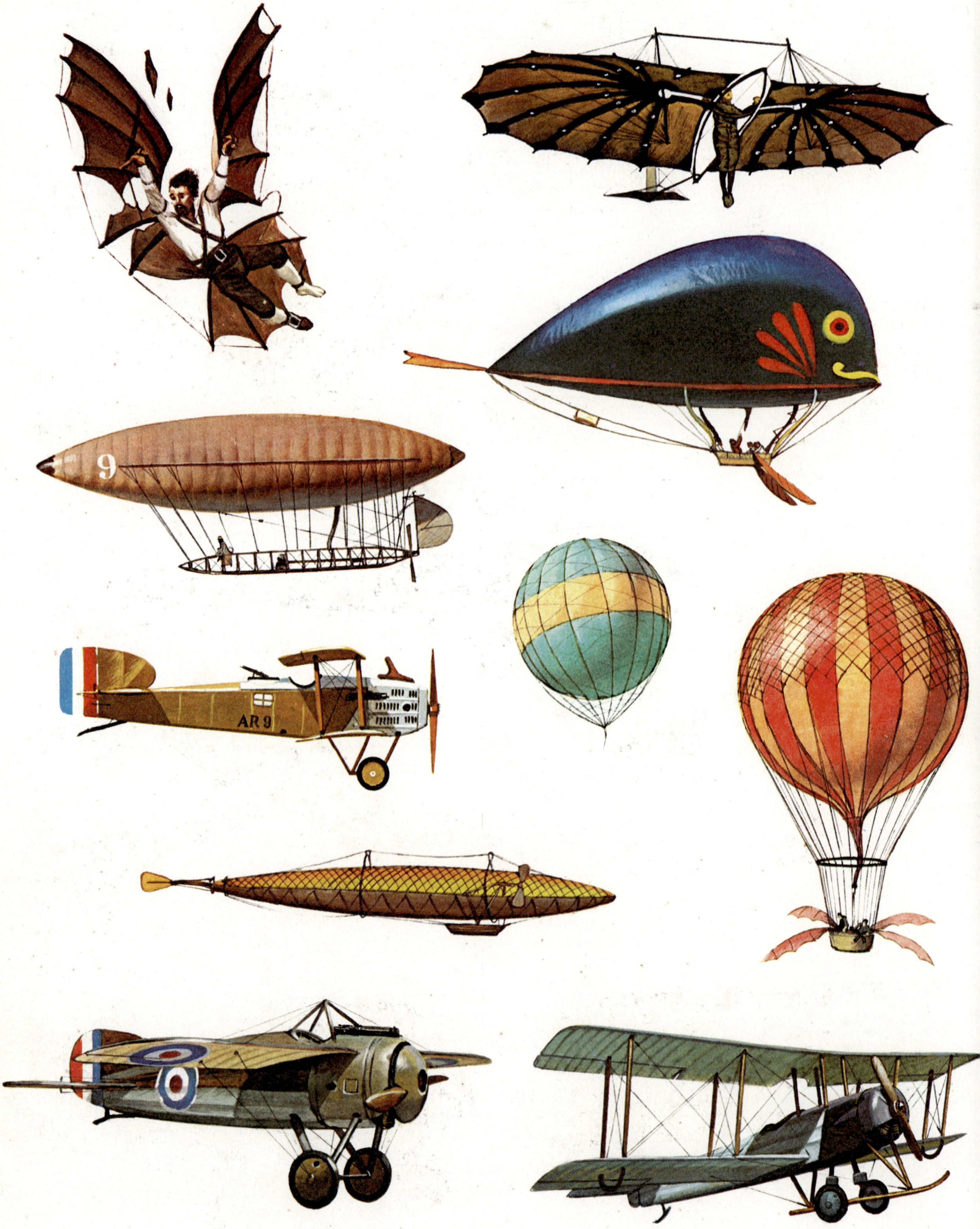
9
AR 9